Tranny Tales

Personal Stories of Gender Transition

Marsea Marcus and
Shannon Weckman, Editors

EQUALITY
PUBLISHING

Library of Congress Cataloging-in-Publication Data

Library of Congress Control Number: 2010940812

Tranny Tales: Personal Stories of Gender Transition /Marsea Marcus and Shannon Weckman, editors.

First Edition

Published by Equality Publishing

www.equalitypublishing.com

ISBN 978-0-9831309-0-1 (softcover)

ISBN 978-0-9831309-1-8 (e-book)

Printed in United States of America

Cover photos are of contributing author, Renee Byers, before and after her gender transition. Photo on right by Matt Levick.

Contents

This book is dedicated to all people who have lost their lives to transphobia, including Gwen Araujo, one of the many undeserving victims. We also dedicate this book to all families of transgendered people in hopes that increased knowledge makes the world a safer place for your loved ones. And finally, we dedicate this book to all transgendered people everywhere, may you have all the support and information you need to create the best life possible for yourself.

Acknowledgments

We wholeheartedly thank each author appearing in this book. It takes a lot of courage to put one's story in print. Most of these authors were driven by a desire to help others by opening up and revealing very personal aspects of their lives. We recognize and applaud each author for their contribution and the effort they put forth in sharing their story with the world. There will be many who will benefit from reading their stories.

We also want to thank Gail Brenner for her excellent editing, feedback and easy-to-work-with style and many thanks to Laura Golden Bellotti and Maren Martin for their finishing touches. To Bruce Lee for his expertise, support and extraordinary creativity, we express our appreciation.

Thank you to Eli Coleman for giving us the little push we needed to keep going.

Shannon's Preface

When I moved to California, in my 40's, I set about trying to learn about myself. I had cross-dressed all my life, which meant I was a transvestite, but now I found myself interested in knowing about transsexuals. After attending cross-dressing socials for over a year, it came to my attention that sometimes transsexuals would attend. This aroused my curiosity, and I approached them at every opportunity to discuss what it was like. I was fascinated by their gender change and began to wonder whether I was a transvestite or a transsexual.

I started seeing a therapist who was knowledgeable about transgendered people. I approached therapy very enthusiastically, reading books and asking lots of questions of the therapist and myself. It was a period of unparalleled personal discovery.

During this time, I gradually came to the conclusion that I was, indeed, a transsexual and that cross-dressing was merely a phase for me. I truly identified more as a woman than as a man. Soon thereafter, I requested a letter from my therapist and began hormonal reassignment.

Although I read many books and articles during this time, very few satisfied my desire to learn more about the experiences of others who had transitioned. Some of the books had been written decades ago. Others were autobiographies, which were limiting in the sense that they were about only one person's experience.

I had tried to reach out to the transsexuals I met at socials, but there weren't many of them. I realized that most transsexuals, upon completing their transitions, were living their lives in their preferred gender role and had no need to continue attending transgender socials. Their lives were now complete where their gender was concerned.

The few transsexuals I did meet were either still considering transition or were in the process of transitioning. What I really wanted was to talk to transsexuals who had completed their transition and were willing to share their experiences. I had lots of questions for them: How was it? Were they happier? Were they glad they did it? How did their families and friends react?

Having completed my transition, I put my own experiences in writing. Some of those writings ended up in transgender newsletters, but the desire to publish and share my transition experiences stayed with me for years, until I met Jamie. Jamie and I both volunteered as speakers for our local Triangle Speaker's transgender program and community outreach. One evening, Jamie invited me and some other people over for dinner. After dinner, I mentioned that it was a wish of mine to write a book about the experiences of transsexuals who had fully transitioned and were living full-time as their preferred gender. Jamie's significant other, Marsea, said that she, too, had been thinking about a similar idea. Soon thereafter we began asking transgendered acquaintances if they would be willing to share their stories in a book. Thus *Tranny Tales* began to take shape.

I hope that the stories in *Tranny Tales* will provide insight and support to those of you who are considering a gender transition, and serve as a source of education for the general population. For many, changing gender is not a choice. They feel so strongly that they must live in their preferred gender role that not doing so may result in extreme unhappiness, depression or even suicide. For others, the unmade decision is like a weight they carry, a strong desire combined with considerable anxiety. My own transition was long and daunting at times, but having completed it, a burden has been lifted and my life is much more rewarding as a result.

When I started transitioning, one daunting question I had was whether I could really be perceived as female. Well, as it turned out, this goal was definitely achievable. We included photos in this book so that readers can see for themselves the dramatic changes in appearance that are possible.

It was a challenge finding other transsexuals who were willing to share their stories and photos. It takes a lot of courage to publicly share something so intimate. I hope that our honest sharing proves both enlightening and valuable to you.

Marsea's Preface

When the man I was beginning to fall in love with told me that he used to be a woman, I was absolutely shocked. How could this bearded, hairy, masculine person ever have been a female? He had previously mentioned that there was something about his past that he needed to tell me. I had worried that he had been in jail or had some kind of legal trouble. So, though surprising, it was also a bit of a relief when he told me that he had been born female.

But I had mixed feelings. I had never known a transgendered person before. What did this mean for me? I had become accustomed to living an open and honest life, free from secrets. Did I now have to live a life of secrecy? If he used to be a woman, did that mean he really was a woman? And what did my attraction to him say about me? Was I really a lesbian?

The only transgendered people I had any familiarity with were either famous (i.e. Renee Richards, Christine Jorgensen) or presented as "weirdos" on Jerry Springer. It never occurred to me that a neighbor, a co-worker, or even my new boyfriend, might be transsexual as well.

In trying to cope with my shock, feelings of betrayal, and fear (what would other people think?), I reflected on the course of my relationship with Jamie, why I liked him, and who he was underneath the façade of body and clothing. I came to the conclusion that, although he had protected himself by avoiding the disclosure of this information earlier, this didn't mean he was a deceitful person. I came to understand how hard it had been for him to figure out when to tell me. I realized that he actually told me as soon as it became necessary that I know. I understood that Jamie didn't want to lose me based on his being transgendered, before I had a chance to get to know him and make an informed decision about whether or not to stay with him.

I stayed.

Jamie relayed to me that his gender change helped him to become more of who he really was. When we met, it was a long-ago part of his past and no longer a big issue for him. I realized that his decision to go through with the change reflected a profound strength of character.

Through Jamie, I met numerous transgendered people, whom I really liked and respected. I came to understand the challenges these friends faced in a world that not only didn't understand them, but could discriminate against them and even feel justified in physically attacking them. Around this time, a young transgendered girl, Gwen Araujo, was murdered not far from my home. It hit me that more stories about transgendered women and men needed to be told.

Those of us who have never had the experience of questioning our gender often find it difficult to separate gender from physiology. If you have ever had a weight problem, however, you may be able to relate to it in this way: If you are overweight the world sees you as fat, makes judgments and stereotypes about you as a fat person, and relates to you based on those perceptions. But you know there is a thin person inside of you, a part of your personality and being that no one sees. You struggle to lose weight so that you and other people will see that person. You may even undergo surgery in your desperation to bring that thin person into the world. You feel that losing weight will restore you to your "real" self. That is what being transgendered is like for some. Except that, in our society, if you lose weight to become who you really are, you are applauded and praised. However, if you change the sex of your body to become your real self, you are very often rejected, ridiculed, or fired from your job and, sometimes, even beaten or killed.

Transgendered people are, first and foremost, people. As you will discover in this book, they love, and they lose love; they have good jobs, bad jobs and no jobs; they have good times in life and bad times. They can be great people and they can be jerks; they have good relations with their families, bad relations and no relations, just like the rest of us. They are as varied in their opinions as any other group of people. They laugh, they cry, get depressed and grieve, and, like everyone else, they have hopes, dreams and disappointments. What is not like everyone else is the challenge they face in making the difficult decision to change their bodies and gender presentation and to live in a world that not only doesn't believe in, understand or accept their choice, but actively hates them for it.

We started writing this book several years ago. At that time there weren't any television shows featuring transgendered people. There were no Oprah-style discussions about transgendered kids and their families; no well-spoken transgendered representatives on the talk show circuit; no public awareness that a transgendered person could be "normal." Now we have Chaz Bono and his excellent book, *Transitions*, and we have movies, reality shows, and interviews with all kinds of transgendered people. The world is finally opening up and beginning to understand that being transgendered is a normal part of our diversity as people.

Transgenderism, like many other physical and psychological conditions, strikes randomly, and it could have happened to any of us. If it didn't happen to you, it can be very difficult to understand. We believe that the varied and compelling stories in this book will shed light on transgenderism in a profoundly personal way. These are stories about people who have gone down the difficult path of introspection, soul-searching, and gender change in order to finally be able to express their true selves—despite the odds and recrimination.

It is our hope that you will learn from and be inspired by this book, and that it will become part of a larger movement to put an end to the violence against transgendered people everywhere.

Introduction

Most people go through life without questioning the gender into which they are born. They accept the fact that they are either male or female, and they rarely, if ever, consider what it would be like to be the other gender. This isn't true for people who are transgendered. Transgendered people tend to question their gender, often from very early on in their lives. They may feel deeply that they are not living in the gender role that feels right to them. They may be very uncomfortable in their bodies, especially after puberty. They may feel like they are crazy because they see themselves differently from how others see them. They may feel like everyone else is crazy, because it's obvious to them who they really are. Although they may not act on it until much later in life, if at all, many transgendered people spend a lifetime questioning, wondering and fantasizing about physically changing their gender.

We compiled *Tranny Tales: Personal Stories of Gender Transition* for people who are looking for information on changing their own gender, for people who have already changed their gender and want to find out about their "comrades" experiences, and for people who are simply interested in why someone would make this choice. This book will give the reader a broad view of the different paths that transgendered people have taken in coming to terms with their gender.

Some transgendered people come to a point where they decide to physically change their bodies to reflect who they truly are. Those who take the step of taking hormones or having surgery are called trans-sexuals.

It takes a lot of courage to be a transsexual, though many would say it was desperation rather than courage that drove them to taking that momentous step. We think it takes courage to use introspection and experimentation to figure out what is really true about yourself and more courage to risk the potential judgment and rejection, and then to live through it. We believe you will agree with us as you get to know the individuals whose stories you're about to read.

As many of the stories in this book reveal, most transgendered people initially try to "fit in." They try to act the part of their assigned gender, sacrificing who they really are and what they really want in order to be "normal" and accepted by their loved ones and society. Sadly, such "acting" rather than "being" usually results in unhappiness or depression.

The process of coming to terms with your gender can take decades. Questioning your authentic gender identity, searching for answers, considering how family, friends, and colleagues will react, and finally, figuring out the physical and financial logistics of a gender change—each of these steps takes time. And everyone's story has its own path and timeline, as you will discover in this book.

Once the long process of changing one's gender has been made, there are social and sexual implications that may affect a person for the rest of their lives. Fortunately, the end result of this long pursuit is that transgendered individuals no longer feel the angst and despair which they have lived with for so long. As *Tranny Tales* shows, most transsexuals end up feeling that their body and mind are finally in sync, which then frees up their energy for other pursuits.

Changing your gender can be fraught with obstacles or it can go quite smoothly. It can be exciting, scary, painstaking, liberating. The stories in *Tranny Tales* illustrate a variety of transsexual experiences. What they have in common is that each of these individuals embarked on a soul-searching journey to figure out who they really are—and each achieved his or her dream of gender transition despite the odds.

Both editors of *Tranny Tales* have intimate knowledge of the transsexual experience. Marsea's life partner is female-to-male and his story is included in this book. Shannon herself is a male-to-female individual and her story is included as well. We hope that the openness of all the people represented herein will allow you to put yourself in their shoes and share in their journeys. We also hope that in learning more about what people go through to change genders, there will be greater understanding and insight about what it means to be transgendered and transsexual.

Tranny Tales shows how self-awareness, perseverance, and creativity can carry people through profound transitions. We hope you will be inspired by the courageous stories in this book—and that you will celebrate in the happiness of those who successfully achieved their dreams to live an authentic life.

Editors' note: Some people have balked at the use of the term "Tranny" in our title, viewing it as a derogatory term. It is our intention to use the term in an affectionate and respectful manner and, by doing so, to remove it from its derogatory context. We find the use of this term to be empowering... and fun! Ultimately, we hope that Tranny Tales contributes to the humanizing of transgendered people and a move away from stigmatizing labels altogether. It is our wish that people who have been offended by this term will join us in embracing it. And if that's not appealing to you, we hope you can forgive us and continue to read these inspiring stories.

Glossary

Alternative community: Refers to a Gay, Lesbian, Bisexual, Transgendered, Questioning Intersexed (GLBTQI) community.

Androgyne, Androgynous: Not differentiated as to gender, a blend of male and female characteristics.

Binding: The act of binding the breasts so they will not be noticed; usually done with an elastic bandage or garment.

Bisexual: Sexual attraction for both men and women.

Butch: Slang for masculine in appearance or manner. Also refers to a lesbian with a masculine appearance.

Cross-dresser, Cross-dressing (CD): A person who enjoys dressing in the gender opposite from their birth gender, but has no desire for a sex change; a transvestite.

Centurion Release (Procedure): An FTM surgical procedure that releases the clitoris into a hanging position and uses the labia majora to create a scrotal sac. This creates the appearance of a penis and scrotum.

Chest surgery: A surgical procedure to remove breasts.

Drag king: A female who performs on stage impersonating a male.

Drag queen: A male who performs on stage impersonating a female.

Electrolysis: The removal of unwanted hair from the body by destroying the hair roots with an electrified needle.

Estradiol: Female sex hormone.

Facial Feminizing Surgery (FFS): A set of surgical procedures to create a more feminine looking face.

Female-to-male (FTM): Female-to-Male, in relation to direction of gender change.

Gender: Refers to a masculine-feminine continuum.

Gender identity: How one perceives themselves on the masculine-feminine gender continuum.

Gender bender: A person who plays with gender presentation; mixing up one's presentation such that they combine or alter male/female characteristics.

Genderqueer: A person who thinks of themselves as both male and female, neither male nor female, or displays an alternative gender presentation.

GLBTI: Gay, Lesbian, Bisexual, Transgendered or Intersexed.

GLBTQ: Gay, Lesbian, Bisexual, Transgendered or Questioning.

Harry Benjamin Standards of Care: The official protocol used by professionals and lay people regarding the sex reassignment process.

Hir: A gender-neutral pronoun that combines the pronouns "his" and "her."

HIV: Human Immunodeficiency Virus, a virus that can cause AIDS.

Homophobia: An irrational fear of homosexuality and homo-sexual individuals.

Homosexual: Sexual attraction toward those of the same sex as oneself.

Hormonal reassignment: The taking of sex hormones in order to change physical sex features.

Hormones: Typically pertains to the male hormone testosterone or the female hormones estrogen or progesterone.

Intersex, Intersexed: The condition of being born with a combination of both male and female physiology.

Male-to-female (MTF):   Male-to-Female, in relation to direction of gender change.

Orchiectomy, orchidectomy: Surgical removal of testicles; castration.

Out: Publicly open about being GLBTI.

Outed: To be publicly revealed, involuntarily, that one is GLBTI.

Packing: Refers to an FTM placing something in their pants to give the feeling and/or appearance of a penis.

Pansexual: A sexual orientation characterized by sexual desire for people, regardless of their gender identity or biological sex; more inclusive of all forms of identity than bisexuality.

PFLAG: Parents, Families, and Friends of Lesbians and Gays.

Polyamorous: The ability to have more than one intimate relationship at a time, with full knowledge and consent of all partners involved.

Premarin: Commercial name for a drug consisting primarily of estrogens derived from a mare's urine.

Purging: Getting rid of the clothing one uses to cross-dress. This is often done periodically to rid oneself of the stress or shame of cross-dressing.

Queer: Originally derogatory slang for homosexual; now in general usage, without negative connotations, as slang to encompass all forms of sexual and gender variations that are outside of the mainstream.

Skank: One who is disgustingly foul or filthy; slang for sexually promiscuous.

Sex reassignment surgery (SRS):   To surgically change one's sex from male to female or female to male. SRS may be partial, for example: an MTF may choose an orchiectomy and forgo a vaginoplasty; an FTM may choose to have a double mastectomy and forgo genital reconstruction.

Spiro, spironolactone: An anti-androgen frequently used to block the male hormone testosterone.

Stealth: Hiding or concealing one's biological sex.

T-blocker: A prescribed drug used to block the effects of testosterone. Frequently used by MTF transsexuals during hormonal reassignment.

Testosterone (or T):   A male sex hormone.

Top surgery, chest surgery: Double mastectomy; a form of SRS for FTMs.

Tracheal shave: Surgical procedure to reduce the trachea making the "Adam's Apple" less noticeable; a procedure frequently done for MTFs.

Trannies: Plural slang for transgender.

Tranny: Slang for transgender. Originally used in porn circles with a sleazy connotation; now used in queer circles with a positive connotation.

Transgender, transgendered, trans (TG):   A general term applied to a variety of individuals, behaviors, and groups involving tendencies to vary from the usual gender roles. This includes transvestites (cross-dressers), people who believe the gender assigned to them based on their genitals was/is incorrect and transsexuals (people who have undergone hormonal therapy and/or sexual reassignment surgery).

Transguy, Transman: Female-to-male person.

Transpeople: Refers to MTF and FTM persons.

Transphobia: The irrational fear of and stigmatization of transgender people because of gender non-conformity.

Transsexual (TS): A transgendered person who undergoes surgery and/or takes hormones to effect a change of sex.

Transvestite (TV): A person who derives pleasure from dressing in the clothes of the opposite sex; a cross-dresser.

Transwoman: Male-to-female person.

Underdressing: Wearing underwear of the preferred gender, while the outer clothes reflect the socially accepted gender.

Vaginoplasty: Surgical procedure that creates a vagina for MTFs.

It Takes
   Courage
      To grow up and
      Turn out to be
      Who you really are.

      e.e. cummings

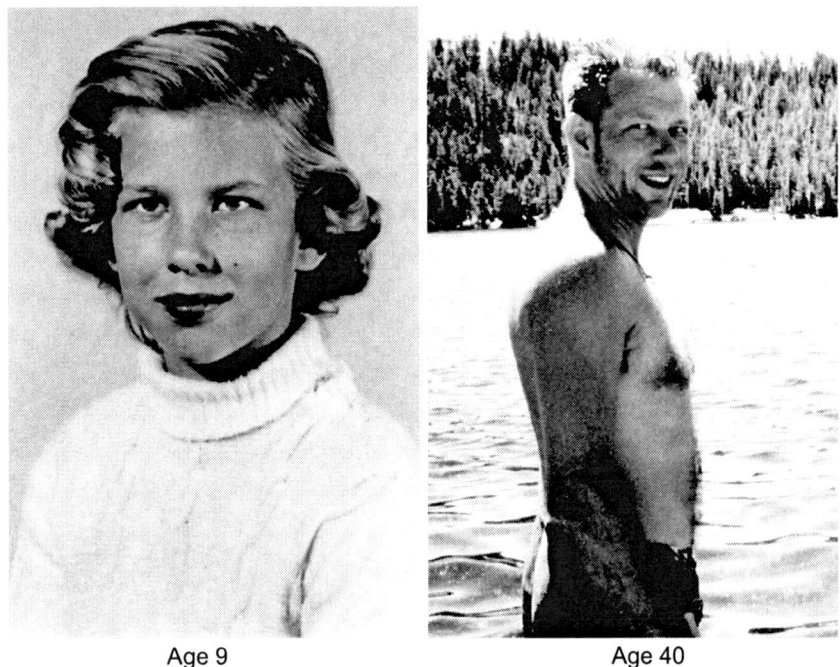

Age 9   Age 40

Jamie is an artist and a musician. He has produced around 50 recordings of original music as a female and over 600 as a male. He and his partner of 15 years live in Santa Cruz, California.

Oh, What a Lucky Man She Was

My earliest recollection of being different from other people was when I was three years old, after having my tonsils removed. They had me in the girls' hospital ward and I couldn't figure out why they would put me in with the girls rather than the boys.

At age four, my brother and I were walking to a babysitter's house and I could see a smoking chimney in the distance. I remember thinking that if the smoke went in one direction it would mean I was a girl and if it went in the other direction, I was a boy. I watched and watched until I saw it go in the direction I wanted... I was a boy!

At my fifth birthday party, which was on a hot summer day, we played outside in the sprinklers. My brother, who was six, took his shirt off and I did the same. My mom told me that girls couldn't take their shirts off. I didn't understand... as far as I could tell my brother and I were the same.

In kindergarten I remember there were blue mats and red mats for assembly. Boys got to sit on the blue mats and girls had to use the red mats. I thought I should be on a blue mat but they told me I had to be on the red. I felt embarrassed that I was put with the girls.

In first grade, I had to wear a dress to school and I was very uncomfortable in it. But winters were very cold where I lived so we got to wear snow pants under our dresses on our way to school. I felt so much better with pants on that even though I would get very hot indoors, I would keep my snow pants on throughout the day. My mother used to get calls from teachers complaining that I wouldn't take my snow pants off.

Throughout childhood, I always wanted to play with the boys. In my opinion, they were more fun. They played with balls and trucks and had sword fights, which I enjoyed. Girls did stuff that didn't interest me like playing with dolls and sitting around talking.

I also loved playing alone. In the bathtub, at about eight years old, I liked to practice shaving my face. I coated my beard area with suds and scraped it off with the rectangle base of a plastic green army man. I used the distorted reflection from the tub faucet in order to see and admire my beard of suds.

In terms of romantic interests, I was always interested in the girls. My first crush was on my third grade teacher. I dreamt of being able to sit with her and hold her hand all day.

In elementary school I was told I had to use the girls' restroom. But I was embarrassed to go in there because I felt I belonged in the boys' restroom. So I avoided it by holding my bladder all day, until I got home. Sometimes I peed in my pants on the way home, but that wasn't as humiliating to me as using the girls' restroom.

When I was nine years old, I started developing breasts. I was extremely disappointed as I realized this meant I really was turning into a girl. I felt God had let me down. I decided to hit myself in the chest with a hammer in hopes of injuring myself and halting the development process. But I gave myself a little practice hit and it hurt! I wanted to injure myself, but I didn't want *pain*!

My mom thought I was a tomboy and this was all just "a phase." I always wanted short hair and she and I used to argue over it. But in sixth grade, Beatles haircuts came in style and, finally, my mom cut my hair in a way I liked. It looked boyish and I was happy.

When I was 12, I cut pieces of hair from my head and glued them on my face for sideburns. It wasn't realistic enough, though, so I quit that. Later when I wouldn't shave my legs, kids teased my brother about it. He complained to my mom and she made me do it for a while.

I enjoyed it when people thought I was a guy. In seventh grade I started counting the number of people I fooled. I stopped counting around 300-something. It meant a lot to me when other people were convinced of my masculinity. But I still had to use the girls' restroom and I hated it, especially when I made the girls uncomfortable. They would think a boy was in their restroom and it would startle them.

I loved gym class but hated dressing and undressing in the locker rooms because I was so uncomfortable in my body. I just hated changing in front of girls. Fortunately, as a teacher's assistant, I was often able to change clothes before or after my classmates.

There was a sense of gender relief when doing sports. In neighborhood softball games it didn't matter what gender one was, the teams were usually selected on ability. I was #1 in my neighborhood among my peers when we played basketball, softball, soccer and especially dodge ball. The ballpark was one place I felt acceptance and admiration. The guys gave me pointers and tips and treated me as if I was one of them.

When my friends first started dating, I was in a real dilemma because I liked girls and people would think I was a lesbian, which was not how I saw myself. I did, however, join the lesbian crowd for a while because I thought perhaps they'd understand me. As it turned out I really didn't fit in with them. In fact, I felt even more alienated when I was with them.

Eventually I started dating a girl who understood where I was coming from. We became friends when I played the male lead in a movie we were making. She understood me... that I was biologically female but was really male inside. I told my mom that my friend Tom and I were going on my first date. I fought with her to let me dress as masculine as possible before letting me out the door. Tom picked me up and played along with my story. Then, as soon as we left, I altered what I was

3

wearing to look even more masculine and then we picked up his female date and mine.

Around age 15 I started binding my breasts when I went out with friends after school. I used my brother's extra ace bandages, which were leftover from his knee injury. I also sometimes brushed mascara on my facial peach fuzz to make it look like whiskers.

Once, when I was 16, I was in a car with my mom and one of my guy friends. My friend referred to me as "James" (which he often called me because he knew I was really a guy) and my mom angrily exclaimed, "We're gonna have to get your hair cut!" I believe what she meant was that I should have it cut in a more feminine style, because my short hair was causing my friend to address me with a boy's name.

Shortly thereafter, she put me in therapy because she was concerned that I was hanging around with the lesbian crowd. After six months, the therapist terminated my treatment because there wasn't anything to do— I was psychologically healthy. Later, when I was in the hospital for knee surgery, Mom had some tests run to see if my hormone levels were off balance. The results showed I was a normal female, but I was still pleased that Mom was looking for underlying medical reasons for my masculinity.

When I was 17, I came across an article in a women's magazine, which my mom bought every Friday. I still remember that it was the May 1973 issue, and the article was called, "My Daughter Changed Sex!" I read about Tracy, the featured transsexual, and realized that's what I was. I felt like I had finally found the key to my life mystery! Around that time I had a 24-year-old girlfriend. She happened to know someone who had had a sex change and she got me the contact numbers for an organization that had helped her friend. I gave this number to my family doctor and told him about the article, explaining that I had always felt I was a guy and that I wanted a sex change. He was very matter-of-fact and willing to help, even though he had never done this before. He got the information he needed and put me on hormones. I know it's a much more complicated process these days, but it was 1974 and at that time there were no Standards of Care, we simply used common sense.

After graduating high school, I wanted to be a commercial artist. I had to go to our local technical institute for training before I could do that work, so I decided I'd go to school while continuing to live at home.

But my mother was remarrying and moving to another state. The next best thing was to move out on my own. Now I could be comfortable living as a full-time male. Diving into the work force seemed easier than trying to manage school without an income, so I went to work and never attended art school.

We lived in Indiana, in the industrial belt that stretched from Chicago to Detroit, and jobs were plentiful. I say this because here I was, presenting myself as an 18-year-old male fresh out of high school, with no work experience, and I had no trouble finding work.

My mom wasn't surprised when I told her I was changing into a man and had begun taking hormones. However, in her words, I broke her heart. Those were sad times. Mom didn't understand me, and she had no one to talk to. Her friends were people of the same religious faith. She tried to confide in another church member but it backfired. Instead of compassion and acceptance, she got misunderstanding and became the subject of rumors. Mom told me she heard of a church member saying my mother must be a homosexual because she bore me. So mom stopped telling others about me and resorted to omitting he/she pronouns when referring to me and only saying "he" whenever I was around because she knew I expected it.

I told a friend my mom didn't approve of my change because she believed the body was the "temple of the Holy Spirit" and that it wasn't for us to alter. My friend said, "Well, you can tell your mom that your temple simply came with the wrong facade." I liked that!

I was 18 years old when the hormones started taking effect. I had just gotten over my adolescent blemishes and here they were starting again! I was working as a male in a neighboring town where no one had known me as female. Unfortunately I got laid off from my first job because I physically could not do the work. But by the time of my second job, also in the same neighboring town, the hormones had really kicked in and strength was no longer an issue.

I loved the changes that were happening to me. I'll never forget the milestone of those first eight hairs on my chin! I didn't talk to my mom much about it because she started becoming more religious and less supportive. But I was proud and periodically sent her photos of myself so she could see how I was changing. Then, she surprised me with a big burst of support.

I was visiting her and I told her that I was binding my breasts with ace bandages. She looked at what I was doing and said she could come up with a much better way to do it. She ended up devising some unique undershirts, or under-vests, that compressed my chest but were padded and sloped in a natural way down my torso. She created five of them for me and I wore them for years.

In 1978 I was 22 years old and moved out West. By this time I had been on hormones for four years and people just naturally referred to me as "he." My old friends and family were slower to let go of my old identity, though, and had difficulty making the pronoun changes. Once, I was having lunch with my mom in a restaurant and she was ordering drinks. She said to the waitress (while nodding toward me), "She'll have a cup of coffee." The waitress looked at me, sideburns and all, and looked back at my mom, examining her a bit closer. I said to the waitress, "I'll have a cup of coffee" and when she left I said, "Mom, you can't continue to call me "she" anymore—people will just think you're crazy!"

Shortly after moving out West, I ran out of hormones. I called some gay organizations and one of them hooked me up with another female-to-male guy. He and I became friends and he referred me to his physician for hormones. He also invited me to parties where I met lots of other people like me. I especially enjoyed meeting couples, not knowing which one was transsexual. It made me realize you can't really tell who anybody is, or was.

A few years later, my mom's "under-vests" were wearing out and I started looking for a plastic surgeon to get rid of my breasts altogether. The surgery was quick and easy. The same friend mentioned above came with me and videotaped it. After the surgery, I felt like I had been relieved of a great burden. I couldn't wait to go to the beach and take my shirt off—in fact I went one week after the surgery. It felt surreal to realize that people had no idea I'd had breasts a week before.

There is not much to report about my transition from that time on. I lived a life like anybody else. I dated a variety of women. I didn't tell them about my history until I could see a long-term relationship was possible. There were a few rejections at that point, which I knew to expect. To protect myself, I never let the feelings get too strong until after I had told them the story and knew they were okay with it. I had several relationships that lasted a couple of years each. They didn't end due to gender issues, just the normal relationship stuff. When I was 39 I met the love of my life and have been with her ever since.

I'm almost 56 years old and I have lived two-thirds of my life as a guy, about 38 years. I made the change at such a young age that I really don't have any idea what it would have been like to live my life as a woman. I don't really consider what I did to be a "sex change," it was more of an evolution into who I really was.

I know in a lot of ways I have been very fortunate, it's not nearly so easy for some trannies to do what I did. I was lucky to have both a first name and a middle name that were gender neutral (Jamie Francis). I was lucky that I was tall. I was lucky that my birth certificate did not have my gender listed on it and my first driver's license didn't have a photo! When I got my driver's license in California, even though my old license said "female," the clerk looked at me with my unshaven stubble, heard my deep voice and listed me as male, no questions asked. She must have thought the old one was an error!

I have wondered about luck, predestined lives and divine intervention ever since I noticed my rocky path as a young female had suddenly become a smooth one, as a tranny. Perhaps one's path is clear when it is the correct path to take.

I have heard many stories about difficult gender transitions and I feel very fortunate that mine was so smooth. Maybe I carry lucky genes. An example of my inherited luck dates back to the early 1900's when my grandmother was emigrating from Lithuania. She and her family saved for a long time to buy one of the last remaining tickets aboard the unsinkable Titanic on its upcoming maiden voyage. She was a short and stout woman who had problems with swelling in her feet so she wore men's shoes, as they were the only shoes that were wide enough for her.

Lithuania was a farm community. My grandmother was dressed appropriately by Lithuanian standards, but on the day of departure she was denied passage because the porter said she wasn't dressed appropriately for first class and her ticket was for a first class deck cabin. The less expensive lower-deck tickets had already been sold out when she purchased her ticket. So my grandmother got off the Titanic with her crates and trunks and was given a refund for her ticket. A few months later she came abroad via another boat and safely arrived at Ellis Island. So perhaps my luck started there!

My biggest problem has been in the area of careers. I think I was late to hop onto the career path because I had to resolve my gender issue before I could really focus on my career path and ever hope to be a productive contributor to this planet. I spent so many years trying to cope with my gender! If I'd had information and support earlier, I wouldn't have had to spend my energies focused on that and could have instead focused on what I wanted to do when I grew up.

On the other hand, perhaps because of my difficulties, I have good coping skills. From a very early age, I used song writing and art to express my feelings and vent my frustrations. This came in especially handy when I got on hormones because one of the first differences I noticed when I started taking testosterone is the effect that hormones have on one's mood. I could no longer cry when I was upset. The feelings were there but my body wouldn't react to the emotion in the same ways it had before. Testosterone provided a drive, an edge, an aggressive quality. As female I had felt anger and frustration. But, on hormones, I felt *rage* for the first time. It took experiencing it to understand why men sometimes act in the aggressive way they do. I don't think people, especially women, fully understand the effect that testosterone has on men.

The sex drive is another example. The biological differences between men and women are incredible. I used to wonder why there were so many prostitutes available for men, but now I understand it. As a female, I wasn't more interested in sex than any other interest. I didn't understand why so many men would act out sexually. As a male, I have found that the sex drive is unbelievably powerful and not easy to ignore or repress, and can be very uncomfortable when not satisfied. After being under the influence of testosterone for a few years, I learned to channel some of this energy into athletics and performing music. Still, the sex drive can be constantly distracting and it can steer my thoughts if I let it.

When the hormones first started taking effect, I really bloomed as a person, both spiritually and physically. Physically, my voice dropped an octave, I developed a nice Adam's apple, my arms and upper body gained muscle and mass, which I aided by working out. My pants no longer fit right because I lost body fat around my butt and gained muscle in my thighs. My breasts became smaller and easier to hide.

Spiritually, I felt alive. My songs took on a happier quality. I felt driven and able to do things I had only dreamed of doing. I felt equal to any other man in a crowd. Women were noticing me in a positive way. And to my surprise, gay men were hitting on me. I was in a relationship with a gay man for a while, but I never got over wanting to be with women and eventually started dating women exclusively.

Currently I am in a long-term, loving relationship with a woman. We have been together for 15 years. The success of our life together is due to the compassion, flexibility and communication she and I put forth. She has been a big part of my growth when it comes to being more open in the world. I tend to be cautious, enjoying low-risk and solitary activities. Aided by her gentle persuasion, I have learned to trust the unknown enough to try things I would never have considered doing in the past. I bring to the relationship a romantic and nurturing spirit. I love taking care of her and making her comfortable. She works late and I enjoy having dinner prepared when she gets home. Which of those traits of hers and mine are gender-based? I don't know and I'm tending to care about it less and less.

For six years, I played bass in a band called Frootie Flavors. We considered ourselves a "Tranny Band" featuring positive songs cel-ebrating our transgendered circumstances. People who came to see us enjoyed the fun atmosphere we created. We sang about the unique situations that come up when you're a transperson, and songs about body parts that have no names because hormones have altered them so dramatically! For example, we had a song about our genitals entitled, "Little Bitty Buddy" and a reggae-style song called "No Tits, No Dick", which used humor to describe the plight of us tranny guys (both songs written by Stu Doogan).

Now that I'm in my 50's, I have menopause symptoms to deal with. I went to my doctor seeking relief and was put on a mild dose of estrogen for a year. After a month I started feeling more mellow than I ever remember feeling. I still had the drive from the testosterone, but, in contrast, I also had a new and constant sense of tranquility. Another effect I noticed was that my body weight shifted and extra fat went to my hips and butt. After realizing that the estrogen wasn't helping my hot flashes and cold sweats, I stopped taking it.

A couple of years ago I saw a nighttime fire-spinning performance. At some point, I noticed that one of the many bare-chested performers was a tranny guy like me, except that he hadn't had chest surgery. I wondered how he had the courage to perform so comfortably in front of thousands of strangers. Seeing his ease and comfort in his body had a tremendous effect on me. I had always been so afraid of ridicule, but what I wanted was this guy's confidence.

More recently, I had the unusual opportunity to go to an outdoor clothing-optional resort in the mountains. I was with four good friends and each of us had our own issues and discomfort with nudity, which we discussed on our way there. Soon after arriving, the other three had removed their clothing and gone off to the pool. I sat on the lawn with shorts on, amidst twenty or so naked people and a couple of other partially-clothed people. I was very uncomfortable.

I feared that once I undressed I would get a lot of attention. I wondered how people would react to what appeared to be a man without a penis. I didn't know if I could handle the stares just yet. How could I possibly be nude and enjoy myself? A loud response popped into my head, "That would take a lot of courage." I immediately burst into tears, which confounded me because it had never happened before. But as soon as I dried my tears, I felt ready to face the world... wearing nothing. I stood up, disrobed and walked through the crowd. Free, like everyone else!

I'm still not sure why I cried and what shifted in my thinking that allows me, to this day, to stand naked among non-transsexual men and women. All I know is that no one made a big deal about it and I had a great time there. And what matters to me more is making similar shifts in other parts of my life. As I mature, I find I am spending less time wondering what other people may think of me and more time accepting who I am and focusing on what I can accomplish. I'm very aware that by just being myself, I educate people. By just being myself I help people broaden their perspectives. And now that I have nothing left to hide, I feel better prepared to tackle the next half of my life.

A while ago, I joined Classmates.com. An old friend contacted me and sent me a summary of her life since high school. She wrote one sentence about each thing. So I wrote back in the same format... "I've been working on music and I did this and that art thing and I moved to California and I had a sex change and I've worked this job and that job..." I just kind of tucked it in there because that's really how it went, a lot happened in my life and that was just one part of it. She responded with the usual: So glad to hear from you blah, blah, blah and "P.S. I always knew you were a guy!"

Age 26   Age 42

Judith (Jude) Russell is a 46-year-old woman living in Hartford, Connecticut with her partner and three dogs. She has been a self-employed electrical engineer since 1995, is addicted to yoga at the time of this writing, and is joyfully welcoming music back into her life. She transitioned on January 1, 2003.

The Scenic Route

Prelude

My transition philosophy has been simple. Transition, for me, was the path I would take if nothing else worked. I was committed to exploring all other options before physically altering my body through hormones, medications, and surgery. And I was not afraid of other people reading me as queer or gay or effeminate or "other" as I explored this side of myself.

I have often likened my transition to slowly wading out into a cold lake. I take a step or two, shiver a bit at the coldness, and hang out for a while as my body acclimates. Then I decide if I want to go deeper. All along the transition I have been open to the concept that I can stay where I am, go back, or push deeper. And though several times I have pulled back—too deep, too fast, too cold—I have always found myself moving toward transition.

As a result of this, my transition has spanned the better part of a decade. It has been a gradual and gentle path. And it has been, in my opinion, a fairly successful one—perhaps in part because of its gradual slope and measured tempo.

Beginnings

The reader will be spared the details of my childhood. Suffice it to say I figured out I was transsexual at an early age. I also figured out that it was problematic to my family and to society. I was glad I had the life skills and guile to be able to hide it. I cross-dressed surreptitiously throughout my childhood and adulthood. As an intelligent and not so athletic young boy, I did not fall into the trap of overcompensation—no military service, no sports hero, no machismo. I was able to survive in the world of men and boys by being witty and smart and quiet when need be, but I was never particularly successful or happy as a male. I remained a virgin until I met my first (and only) wife, Jane. To try to understand why I was not attempting to get her into bed like every other male she had dated, she had to schedule a meeting with a written agenda (we were pretty funny together).

That I did not tell Jane of my gender issues prior to getting married is perhaps the most grievous sin and regret of my life. I had honestly thought that my gender issues were the result of being somehow misguided or on a wrong path and that I had been pulled back on track by her love and our relationship. We married in 1987—a storybook Catholic wedding complete with a Bishop presiding, the newlyweds singing "Grow Old with Me", and a rockin' reception featuring a swing band and a jukebox full of classics. But by 1989, my discovery of cross-dressers and transsexuals online (the word transgender was new and rarely used back then) and our newlywed issues around sex and intimacy had culminated in my blurting out the truth about my gender feelings. Jane was shocked, and my dishonesty doomed our marriage. She eventually moved on with her life, and agreed to keep my secret, but she remains wounded by the experience. The pain I caused her, and my guilt over it, remains a regret that has influenced much of my subsequent journey. I would not find a serious relationship for another decade—long after my transition was in full swing. But I remain alert to the needs of spouses, who are often the secondary victims of a transgendered life.

Therapy

When my confession about cross-dressing started the deterioration of my marriage, I began to go to counseling. In therapy, my cross-dressing and transgendered feelings were out in the open from the start—but I was trying to figure out how to cope with them in the context of a male identity and life. I was certainly not seeking to transition—only to understand, to accept, to heal, and to grow.

I spent three years in various types of therapy—individual, mixed groups, and men's groups. It was good work, and I emerged from the process a more whole person who understood the nature of and the fallout of hir[1] transgenderism, even as I was not yet willing or able to deal with the issue directly. In that way I think that perhaps my journey is different from others I have met; I went deep and dealt with my mother, my father, my family, my religion—all of the social and cultural issues that colored my psyche much earlier than my eventual exploration of my transsexualism.

I emerged from therapy committed to a life of exploration, of openness to change, and of continued growth. Even as I lived for a few years more as a man in touch with his sensitive side, I was slowly coming to terms with the fact that my enlightenment and salvation would be only through the valley of my transsexualism—and that I would not be able to stop, go back, or avoid this subject if I were to remain on a path of truth. I would emerge on the other side as something—a wiser man, a transitioned woman, a sage, a crone, a shaman. But I would not get to where I needed to be by ignoring my transsexualism.

---

[1]   Hir—a gender-neutral pronoun (his / her).

15

Dead Fathers

In 1979, at the age of 18, I became a member of the "Dead Fathers Club." My 44-year-old father succumbed to a life of stress, alcohol use, smoking, a sedentary lifestyle (and perhaps of some of his own repression) and died during an angiogram, following a series of heart attacks.

My father's fate hung over me for the next 20 years. As the oldest son, most likened to him in temperament and physique, I felt as if my fate were written. "You will die young, and nothing you can do will prevent this," my inner voices whispered. I lived with this through much of my young adult life. With the expectation of a young death, I perhaps started my mid-life crisis early, in my mid 20's.

Today, as a transitioned woman, I do not think often of my father. I am not sure how he would react to his new daughter; although I think in his thoughtful logic he would probably have been able to accept hir path.

And, although I know that life is full of the unexpected and unplanned, today I have faith in myself to live a long and healthy life.

Outed

In 1994, Jane came back into town from the West Coast to be with her dying father. Our breakup had caused quite a stir in our community; there were many who blamed her for apparently choosing career over marriage, not aware of the role that my secret had played in tearing us apart. Hoping for some understanding and healing from her family and friends, she told a few people the truth about her former husband. Word spread.

Shortly thereafter, I started to come out on my own to close friends. Each person I came out to nervously listened, nodded, sympathized, reassured me that it was okay, and toward the end of the conversation, confessed, "I already knew…" By the third or fourth such experience I came to the realization that there were not many people in our town who did not know. In fact, a gay male friend of mine reported that a notorious local busybody and gossip, had excitedly told him all about it, not knowing that he was gay nor that we were friends. So… I was an *out cross-dresser*.

The irony is that when all this occurred I was just starting to explore it all myself and had not, in fact, done much in the way of actual cross-dressing. But through the subsequent years, I was blessed with the tacit understanding that "they all know anyway," so I never was particularly shy about people noticing things—shaped brows, long nails, shaved legs, long hair—that some more closeted cross-dressers fret about.

My Chorus

On September 29, 1994, I went to see a woman speaking at Real Art Ways, in Hartford, CT. It's an important date for me—so meaningful that I actually expended some energy tracking it down to include here. The woman was the "Gender Outlaw"—transsexual author, playwright, and work-in-progress Kate Bornstein.

I often describe seeing Kate as the moment I turned around and embraced the dragon that had been chasing me my whole life. Nerdy me, a suburban gender-conforming young man trying to emulate urban hip in chinos, a tweed jacket and loafers in a room full of genderqueers, I was equal parts fascinated and scared to death. Too fearful to purchase her book that night, I eventually did buy one, which Kate lovingly inscribed in crayon many years later.

To this day, Kate remains a part of my journey. I go to see her whenever she is speaking or performing nearby. She has a knack for coming to town when I am at critical life moments—starting therapy or hormones or transition, or struggling with some related issue. I was fortunate to be able to speak to her one-on-one the last time I saw her and I got to thank her for her unwitting role in my journey. My life is better for her being there—perhaps my life is saved for having encountered her. I think of her as my Chorus—she appears onstage between acts in the play that is my life, summing things up, explaining the plot, providing guidance or foreshadow or warning of dire risk. I try hard to listen.

Other Supports

I joined a local transgender support group, the cryptically named Connecticut Outreach Society (COS) early in my process. The people that I met there, the safe space to make mistakes in presentation and performance of gender, and the greater GLBTI[2] community that this group opened up to me have been instrumental in the success of my journey. While I have tended to avoid more social trans events, I remained active in COS throughout my transition.

I have also found support in individuals that I met online and in real life. These peers and mentors have ranged across the spectrums of gender and sexuality—gay men, lesbians, cross-dressers, transsexuals, androgynes, mystics, activists, men, women, friends. I cherish these persons who I look up to and go to for support and advice.

Angels Watching Over Me

I have never been a particularly religious person. Raised a Roman Catholic, I was an altar boy, received the sacraments, attended Catholic school. However, my religious beliefs were measured and more of duty and approval, than deep and mystical. My mother remains a more formal Catholic—hewing to the party line and playing by the rules laid out by the church, colored by her own gentle accepting nature. My father communicated a quiet belief that was equal parts faith and duty. He conveyed to me that there were many paths to the truth; and that he was simply following one of these paths as best he could.

I grew up with a belief in a God, but without a strong sense of faith or devotion to the Christian faith exclusively. Yet, over time, I have become aware of the fact that my journey has been guided and protected by some higher power or life force. When I have found myself on the edge of chaos, a gentle hand pushes me lightly toward stability. When I have needs, sustenance is provided. I have heard that when the student is ready, the teacher appears, and this seems to be true for me.

---

[2]   GLBTI—Gay, Lesbian, Bisexual, Transgendered, Intersexed. Add one more initial and I stop using the acronym and start using the more succinct "Queer"!

I have come to trust in, and in fact to seek out and expect, this sort of protection. It is a quiet and curious belief, part Buddhist, with an awareness of the dance of dark and light and an ability to step back and see the beauty of the entire journey. It includes a divine force—a god, a higher power, a life force that is both protector as well as mischief-maker. I watch the waves and rhythms of the world, and try to ride these waves as best I can.

More than anything else in my journey, the positive feedback that this life force has provided me has convinced me of the rightness of my path. At each milestone, a barrier was encountered, and was removed or overcome by some subtle angel—usually a person, entering my life with resources, support, wisdom, or friendship.

At the age of 42, as I stepped lightly over the barrier between male and female, I found myself having become a mystic. It is an identity I continue to explore.

Gender Blur and Androgyny

One of the possibilities that I considered when I was searching for a way to exist short of transition was the world of gender blur and androgyny. Soon after I started to make contact with the local cross-dressing group, I began to skew my appearance and let my hair grow. My eyebrows were thinned and then shaped gradually into a girlish arch. I shaved my legs and got my ears pierced. I began to wear colors that were not quite so butch. The process was gradual, taking years.

By the time I actually transitioned in 2003, it was difficult for me to be read as a male regardless of my clothing or demeanor. I had to clearly declare my male gender (via male voice) when encountering clerks or waitpersons in business settings to avoid the inevitable and somewhat discomforting, "May I help you, Ma'am?" especially while trying to maintain a coherent male identity among clients and professional peers.

Yet when I transitioned, my family, friends, and co-workers were surprised. My mother had fretted about my long hair for years, and my pierced ears had caused a small flurry of concern—but until I transitioned, people chose to ignore that I was changing my gender presentation. My male gender presentation was in other ways (behavior, voice) unambiguous, and taken for granted.

In actuality, when January 1, 2003 rolled around and I transitioned, there was very little that was different about me. My hair was the same—a bit more nicely kept perhaps. My clothes were not all that different. I wore very little makeup thanks to years of electrolysis. I simply removed the male gender cues and behaviors that had been propping up my male identity, and stopped trying to disguise my nascent breasts. I was a softer, more colorful, and expressive version of me. From a physical perspective, transition was almost a non-event.

Relationships

When I was young I did not date. I was too wounded and socially inept, plus my cross-dressing and transgendered feelings overwhelmed any natural desire for relationship and sex.

To be honest, NOT being in a relationship was very important to my transition process. I needed the space and relative calm that being alone brings. Imagine a fish in a still pond—able to swim freely and safely and explore all corners of the pond equally. I liken my exploration to this; I needed the freedom to poke around a bit, to see what was out there and who I really was. I did not need the feelings and opinions of others to muddy the waters.

I have watched transgendered friends, seemingly on the verge of transition, who meet, mate and marry more conventionally gendered partners. They often return to the closet, miserable, living with perpetual tension in their relationships. It's difficult to watch—like a car crash in slow motion. You just wait for the noise, the broken glass, and hope the participants emerge without too many injuries. For these reasons, I had pretty much resigned myself to being alone.

After my marriage, I shied away from relationships for many years—feeling too guilty over my role in hurting Jane, and not quite sure where I was headed. When I did finally start dating, I kept it light and non-intimate, and chose partners that were suitably liberal and queer-friendly. After I started actively exploring my cross-dressing, I told all of my potential partners about it up front. However, I did not have a significant, committed relationship from 1990 until 2000, when I met my present partner Alex.

In March of 2000, I was staffing an information table for a CD/TG group at a GLBT Youth Conference. A lesbian-looking woman approached with a tale of her transsexual girlfriend, her life in Oregon and Washington State, her recent move to Connecticut. I talked with her politely for a while before sending her over to another group's table. I perhaps waved to her once more at the conference, but that was it.

My first impression was well-founded. The woman, who I later came to know as Alex, was indeed a lesbian-identified woman (although her history might be better described as bisexual) who had come to find herself attracted to the blend of energies and genders that she found in transsexual women. What I did not pick up on at the conference was her interest in *me*. She had read me as full-time female at the conference (though I wasn't at the time) and she tracked me down online afterwards and asked me out via email.

Less than a year later we moved in together, and remain together today. Without a doubt I would have had a rougher transition without her support and encouragement, and without the security and financial safety net that being part of a couple provides. Our relationship is unconventional—we are committed and cohabitating but are also polyamorous. I find the hormones and testosterone suppressants to be a bit libido-crushing, so I am not all that interested in other partners. But if that time should come, we are open to it. And truthfully, my sexuality seems to shift and flow as I transition.

Working

Work is important. Without it there is no money and without money there is no transition. Transsexualism is a game best played by the wealthy. It is not fair and it is not right that this is so. But in the United States of America at the start of the 21st century that is the way it is. My advice: stay employed.

I spent my early work life bopping around at various electrical engineering jobs. In 1989, I started to work for a large medical imaging company as a national Power Quality Specialist. In fact, I informally became known as the "Power Guy," as in "I think there is a power guy up in the national office who might be able to help with this." It was a dream job. I developed a reputation as someone who knew what they were doing and was good at it.

In late 1995, amid a market downturn, my company needed to downsize and they offered me a pretty decent separation package. I had been talking about starting my own consulting practice for years, and leapt at the chance to get out on my own. It was the best thing I could have done for my transition. Truth be told though, I was not planning to transition in 1995. I was starting to explore my gender issues, however, and knew that I could use a little bit of breathing room outside of the corporate world. Eight years later I remain self-employed and have been able to transition on the job. I lost exactly *one* major client through my transition.

I have just a few bits of advice to offer to those seeking to transition in the workplace:

• Diversify. When transition became a possibility I started to diversify my work, seeking other types of work that might be a bit more open to a woman (and a transsexual woman at that) than the field service, male-dominated, ex-military world of my engineering clients. Even if you are employed, learn new skills that might be useful for the newly gendered you.

• Do not come out too early. I did not tell any of my clients until a few weeks before my transition. That they may have guessed or read me as gay was not a surprise to me, but they were willing to keep it professional as long as I was. Once I transitioned and a few months had passed, my transition was not spoken of all that much. I have witnessed transgendered persons who have come out at work just weeks or months into their journey, and I think, "Are you sure you want to live with this for the next two to three years before you are actually able to transition?"

• Have patience and humor. I have, in all areas of my life, been exceptionally patient with those who inadvertently butcher names and pronouns. People are sufficiently comfortable with me to be able to say "Mike" and "he" accidentally and not feel mortified—and as a result they try very hard to get it right. I can laugh about my predicament and have sympathy for the non-transpersons I interact with for whom this is very unusual and unconventional. I cut them slack so long as their gaffes are not malicious.

Getting a Life

It was very important for me to escape the shelter of the transgendered community, and to explore my female identity without the politeness and political correctness of persons who are familiar with transsexuals. My transition was aided by some non-transgendered groups that were accepting and safe spaces for me to test whether or not I could actually pull off a transition.

Folk Festival: In 1991 or so, soon after my separation, I stumbled across a small folk music festival in New York. I signed on as a volunteer despite knowing no one there and being alone. I went, camped out, worked, met people, and had a wonderful time. I have returned each year and it has become something I now consider a retreat, a vacation, family, and sacred space. And slowly, I transitioned in this world.

In my questioning days I tried out new identities at the festival, experimenting with feminine accessorizing, leaning toward the more queer or more androgynous in my presentation. The few years prior to my transition, I began to spend my festival weekend in more female spaces. The left-leaning, earthy crunchy, queer-friendly folkies were a perfect test for my eventual transition. And, of course, I loved the brightly colored folk music dresses.

Ballooning: One of my housemates' boyfriends was a hot air balloonist. Noticing the propane tanks strapped to the bed of his pickup I asked, "So… are you a welder?" Thus began 20 years of balloon crewing.

Crewing for a hot air balloonist is generally an unpaid activity. One gets up at 5:00 a.m., helps to inflate the balloon, drives the chase vehicle, and helps to pack up the balloon. There is champagne and breakfast afterwards, friendship, camaraderie, a lot of fun, and occasionally a chance to go for a free ride. It is a wonderful experience.

At the end of the 2001 flying season, my gender ambiguity had reached a point of distraction. Passengers and passersby were referring to me as "she" as often as "he." I recall a festival where, post flight, another female crew person and I jokingly draped ourselves across our pilot's MG sports car, champagne glasses in hand. A passerby whipped out a camera to capture "two girls who know how to live." And, at the same time, I was still trying to pass as a man!

Not wanting to cause problems for my friend the pilot (what was a hobby for me was his livelihood), I spoke to his girlfriend and then to him about my transgenderism. As a result, I transitioned in the ballooning world about nine months prior to my official transition.

Again, this afforded me the opportunity for self-evaluation. As I interacted with passengers, other pilots, and strangers at the landing sites and breakfast haunts, I could ascertain for myself whether or not I had the skills, the presentation, and the chutzpah to identify and live full-time as a woman.

There were complications, of course. With no formal announcement, my transition hit the streets via the grapevine. I recall one fellow crew member inquiring on the balloon crew radio band, "So, Jude... what's with the name change?" as 30-40 pilots, crew persons, and passengers listened in. "It's a long story, Ellen..." was the best I could come up with; but I got her up to speed later that day, without the benefit of a radio transmitter!

Aerobics: I had never really been much for exercise. But in the fall of 2001 I discovered aerobics. I had looked into aerobics classes in years past—as a way to exercise and perhaps explore some more female space, while I was living as a male, but there was no place close or convenient and I dropped the idea. When I moved in with Alex I stumbled across a class nearby, and started to go. I went androgynously—introducing myself as "Jude" and not really declaring gender in either my clothes or affect—no makeup, no overt breasts. This particular aerobics class was officially co-ed, though in reality it was almost entirely women. I felt safe exploring this space because, since men were welcomed, they could not object to me as a man, only as a gender transgressor.

I slowly realized I was considered one of the women. Though the leader often exclaimed, "Looking good ladies!" I didn't know for sure until she yelled, "Ladies... and Jerry" for the benefit of a visiting husband.

More confident, I gradually dressed less ambiguously, adding small breast pads, and became one of the girls. Aided by many hours of electrolysis and a full head of hair, which permitted me to go sans makeup and wig, I nevertheless remained somewhat reserved in the classes for fear of offending. But this gym (as well as 8-10 other franchises I have visited across the country) seemed to have no problem

24

with me. And the exercise was and is wonderful for me mentally, physically, and emotionally, as I grow more comfortable with my female physiology and identity.

I hold no conceptions that I am stealth or passing in the aerobics world—only that my presentation is acceptably female and my presence is not disruptive.

These three spaces—folk festivals, ballooning and aerobics—were the crucibles in which I developed my female identity and proved to myself that transition and living full-time were within reach.

An Out Transsexual

Stealth was never a particularly good option for me. I work in a field that is small and specialized, with only a few dozen people working in my specialty at my level. So disappearing and popping up elsewhere as a full-time female was not a practical option. Also, I have become embedded in many social circles and relationships that I would choose not to abandon. I like to be a fairly low-maintenance dresser, and I am a taller and larger woman, and I just don't want to work as hard on my gender presentation as it would take to qualify as stealth. Also, my family has been accepting and supportive, and I choose to remain close to them and integrate them into my professional and social worlds. So I prefer an absence of secrets.

I do not go out of my way to affect a hyper femininity, nor do I shy away from discussions about my past. If people ask, I tell. I assume that most people can tell that I am transsexual through our interactions, although sometimes I am surprised. In my experience, most people choose not to ask. My gender presentation and gender cues seem to be sufficient for them to consider me female. That's all I ask.

As part of a lesbian couple with a partner who is also fairly gender transgressive (her identity extends to her shaved head and a pick-up truck covered with alternative bumper stickers), I am not likely to live my life as a mainstream heterosexual woman. And the people that I most respect in this world—whether trans, queer, or straight—live with the honesty, integrity, and woundedness of an "out" life, so that is how I need to live as well.

Fini

I do not profess to be an expert at transition. It is a difficult path that each person must carve out for hirself, using hir unique skills, experiences, and goals. What worked for me might help you in your journey, but it also might not.

Go gently, go slowly, take your time. Transition is a life journey, and it does not end—ever. There are milestones—self-acceptance, coming out, hormones, transition, and reassignment surgery. But none of these marks the end of the journey. Only death—that final transition—will mark the end of your journey as a transgendered person. Until that time—enjoy the life, enjoy the journey.

Still on the Scenic Route

It has been over three years since I wrote the first part of this story. Much has changed, since then, and much is the same.

I remain transitioned. That has not changed.

I am still with Alex, my partner—we've been together six years, five cohabitating. Our relationship continues to amaze me. With the drama of my transition fading, we continue to work on relationship stuff, including her own struggles with gender and now also with her health. We go to a support group for one of her medical issues and it's nice to be the supportive spouse for a change.

I remain self-employed and my professional life has grown. My diversification strategy during transition, while prudent, proved to be unnecessary. I've gained new clients and new projects. My transition seems to hardly touch my professional life these days. Every so often I get a call from someone who had not heard, who is looking for the old me, or who is making first contact. But for the most part, my transition is old news.

Another special angel came into my life, although I am not sure I realized the significance at the time. At a transwomen weekend a woman handed me a piece of paper with the name Marci Bowers on it. At the time, Dr. Bowers was a fairly obscure surgeon learning about transsexual surgery from Dr. Stanley Biber. I did some research, found mention of her website online, and wrote to her inquiring about bottom surgery, which I assumed to be years off. I also mentioned the fact that I did a little bit of web design work. A few months later I had a surgeon, and she had a webmistress. I'm honored to have been working with Dr. Bowers (on her website) since 2003, watching with delight as her practice and reputation has grown. In December of 2003, I took my own trip to see her in Trinidad, Colorado for genital surgery. To this date, Dr. Bowers remains a friend and a very special angel to me, as well as to many others.

My faith that resources and people will come into my life as I am ready for them and need them remains firm. Again and again, I have found support, adventure, and sustenance to be available, if only I am patient, acknowledge my needs, and watch for opportunities.

Genital surgery is often seen as the terminus of many MTF transition stories, followed by "happily ever after." I have viewed mine somewhat differently. I believe that as we have spent years climbing up the mountain in order to transition, we need to spend a similar amount of time climbing down the mountain afterwards.

The year following my surgery was a difficult one; I battled lethargy and mild depression. Perhaps these were related to the effects of surgery and anesthesia, perhaps to the achievement of a major life goal. I also came to the realization that growing up trans had been traumatic in many ways, and it was only once I was safely transitioned and no longer needed my strength and armor to survive that I could let myself begin to feel the pain.

One way I have found healing is through yoga. While I continue to do aerobics, I stumbled across a small yoga studio a little over a year ago. In the subsequent months I came to find yoga to be my new therapy, as I began to communicate with a body that I had been disconnected from for most of my life. I suspect yoga shall remain a part of my spiritual and physical regimen for the foreseeable future.

Music is another important aspect of my life today. I have been an amateur musician most of my life—playing guitar at church and at open mics. When my father died, I tucked a guitar pick into his suit pocket at the funeral home. Music has been important to me, but in some ways I felt as if music was the price I paid to transition. The energy of transition left little time for music, and my own doubts and fears of performing in public as a woman had kept me away. It seemed as if it might be gone for good.

Recently, however, it has come back into my life. I received a bouzouki (an eight stringed instrument of Greek origin, often used in Celtic music) for a birthday present and I am learning how to play it. I have also started to play guitar with the ensemble that leads periodic Kirtan (chanting) events at my yoga studio. As I have spoken of this to friends, they smile with approval. While I did not see the significance of music in my life, many of them had, and had noted its absence. The fact that music is back in my life feels affirming and significant.

There are those who will say, "I used to be transsexual, but am no longer. Now I am a (wo)man." I do not hold that belief. For me, transsexualism is like a disease in remission—I live with the scars and wounds of this experience. I remain watchful for fallout, and I am dedicated to spiritual, emotional and physical health in light of both my transsexual history and perhaps my fragility as a woman and as a human being. I view my transsexualism as a "felix culpa", a happy fault, which has been the catalyst for my spiritual growth. So while being transgendered is no longer the core issue in my life, it remains an important aspect of my identity.

I've become involved in the True Colors mentoring program. (True Colors, is the GLBTI youth conference where I met Alex). In 2005 I was matched as a mentor with a 17-year-old transwoman. My role with her varies—big sister, alternate parent, transgender resource, driver, and friend. She has many more challenges in her life than I ever had, and we explore the similarities as well as the differences in our experiences. I am honored to share her journey and help out as I can. Many transsexual men and women disappear following transition; yet there are so many ways to give back and help out. Mentoring and working with trans youth seems to be the path that works for me.

A few months ago, I took my young mentee to a book reading to see and hear Kate Bornstein, who remains my unwitting chorus. It was pretty special. I stood at the back of the room and watched my charge shyly speak to Kate and get her book signed, and it felt like the torch had been passed. Although Kate and I did not speak that night, except to exchange hellos, it felt like energy was passed. I hope that she knows how deeply she has touched my life. If not, "Thanks Kate."

When I came back from my surgery trip in early 2004, I dove into the local transsexual support group, which had been slowly dying (at times there were just three or four of us at meetings). I was hoping to help revitalize it, make it more accessible to youth, to persons of color, to those with less in the way of money and privilege. I think we have had some limited success—the group is in better health today. I then become aware of the issue of "male" privilege in the transgender community, with transsexual women of my experience, age, and background tending to dominate the discourse at support group meetings. So, though I was a local leader, I stepped back and became less visible, in hope that other stories might be told, other faces seen and voices heard.

I now sit at the keyboard a slightly different person. More humble, perhaps. Happier. Still curious about what comes next. And I am still enjoying the scenery.

Travel gently friends. Namaste!

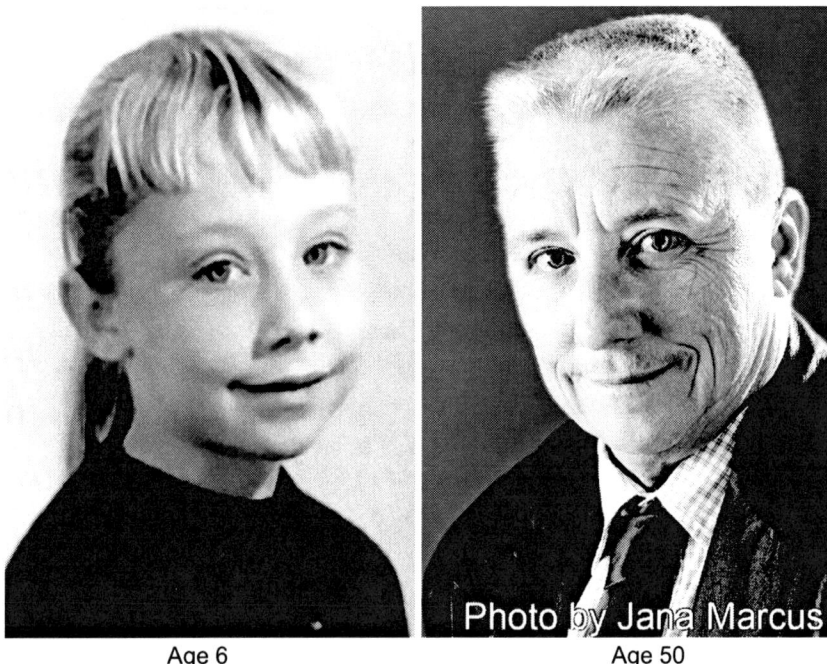

Age 6   Age 50

Owen Wolf is a 58-year-old man currently living in Seattle, WA. He is a performing arts technician, working in live theater as a stagehand, props artisan, scenic painter, costumer and sound technician.

Becoming a Son

Part I

I told my mother in August, a month after my fiftieth birthday. She'd driven two hundred miles to come for a week's visit, a break from the loneliness of a widow with grown children. She's a young seventy. I was her first, born when she was a nineteen-year-old who wanted nothing more in 1952 than to be a mother. I know it didn't come as much of a shock, but now that the words were out, she looked off into space, her face twitching slightly, her hands toying with the corners of the magazine that lay in her lap. I found myself holding my breath.

"Well, if that's really what you need to do to be happy…" Her voice was thin, dispirited, almost disembodied. Not at all her usual. The words hung between us as I waited for whatever tack she might take from there. She took a deep breath, then, in a more cheery tone, asked, "What time does the quilting workshop start in the morning? What do we need to bring with us?" I weighed my reaction. Relief and disappointment. A moment of doubt—had she heard me? Had she understood the magnitude of what I was telling her? What more did I expect? Had she heard the pain in my voice, the determination, the relief? Or did she hear the doctor's voice, fifty years in the past, telling her she had a healthy baby girl?

"Bring the usual stuff, Mom," I said, momentarily resigned, "All your usual tools and supplies." I was breathing again. The voice in my head was telling me I'd done what I needed to do and should leave it alone for now. Give her some time. "You realize," my voice sounded even higher than usual, though I struggled to keep it in the lowest part of my range, "the women at the workshop are going to treat me as male. A lot of them have only known me as a man." The voice in my head, deep and clear, kept saying "Let it go. That's enough for now." I clamped my jaw, willing myself silent.

Mom fidgeted a bit. The impulse to try to insulate her from the hurt was like a bubble in my chest, pressing hard. I argued with myself that she'd accepted me through my high school years, dressing in boys' jeans and men's shirts, wearing cut-offs and a T-shirt under my graduation gown. And when I'd clung to that mode of dress through much of my adult life, she'd continued to accept me. She accepted me after the divorces, and when I'd fallen in love with a woman, when I'd called myself a lesbian, and through my ten years as a Butch. But now, she wouldn't even look at me. In my boots and jeans, my plaid button-up shirt and the tight silver-gray flat-top, I looked a lot like my father. "Mom, I've told you before. It's not your fault. It's nothing you did. It's who I am, who I've been since I was a little kid. I've never been like Lori and Jen." Her eyes darted from side to side in her motionless face. She was remembering, images of three little girls flashing in her head. She sighed.

"I need to get the rest of my things out of the car." She laid the magazine on the seat of the chair and moved toward the door.

32

Part II

"Oh, she'll help me if I get confused," Mom said, gesturing toward me. Her voice was tense, with the sing-song, falsely cheerful lilt that belies her anxiety in a group of strangers. But there was no edge of malice in it. We sat in front of sewing machines with piles of odd colored fabric squares between us. Hearing that, my jaw clenched, and I felt the heat creep into my face yet again. Three days of classes and lunches with forty strangers had been stressful. Mom is uncomfortable in groups, afraid of looking the fool, of attracting attention.

I watched the instructor at the front of the room. Her eyes darted to me, and then back to my mother. In the past three days the instructor had vacillated between "he" and "she" as she referred to me. Today, it seemed, she had found a comfortable solution to the curious dilemma, her voice betraying no hesitation in her choice of references to me— "she" when she spoke to my mother, but "he" when she spoke to anyone else. She even commented on how nice it was to see a man in her quilting classes. Comment notwithstanding, I couldn't help but notice that nearly all of the other ladies who had originally accepted me as Owen on the first day were referring to me as "she" by that last day.

We worked until the end of the afternoon, and then set about cleaning up. The instructor stopped at our table to chat. We were discussing my quilts and how I'd come to work with fabric. I handed her my business card, and invited her to look at my website. She smiled and mentioned how she liked my name... Owen. I smiled. I almost always smile when I hear someone call me by name.

"She'd kill me if I told you her *real* name." The voice from just over my shoulder held a tone that passed for teasing to the uninitiated ear, but I felt it as a slap.

The instructor stood, wide-eyed, watching as I stammered a few syllables, then, unable to make a coherent response that would not be rude and embarrassing to all of us, I turned and walked away from the table without another word.

Part III

On a chill November day, we sat at the table over one last pot of green tea. The server laid the tab at my elbow and retreated in silence. Marla was a big, friendly woman in her sixties. She and I hadn't taken time to get together for lunch in weeks. We often used the time to discuss our lesson plans for the sewing classes we teach together or just to have some time to talk about kids, projects and life. She seemed distracted, a little nervous as she swirled her tea in the heavy oriental cup cradled in the palm of her hand. I watched her in silence, my own cup held between my palms, welcoming the warmth.

"I don't know if I should say anything," she started gently, her eyes on the cup in her hand. Then plowed ahead, "but your mother kind of did a number on you at Summer Workshop." My mind shot back to the last day at lunch, when mom and I had gone late to the dining room and found ourselves at separate tables at opposite ends of the room. I'd sat down to a lunch I hardly tasted, doing my best to stay engaged in the conversations at my table. Marla reached for the teapot.

"I need to hear it," I sighed then straightened my shoulders.

"I just feel so bad, telling you..." Tea splashed on the white tablecloth as she poured.

"Mar, we've been friends for years. I'd rather hear whatever it is from you than from someone else and I'd certainly rather know what's out there than not."

"Well, it wasn't *that* bad, but she just went on and on about your house. How it's a mess and you just don't care about anything." She dabbed her napkin at the tea stain on the tablecloth.

"That's all? That my house is a mess?" I nearly laughed with relief. "She didn't say anything about my transition? About my 'pretending to be a man'?" Marla managed a weak smile, shaking her head, no. I forced a smile, but it didn't change the heaviness in my voice. "We email three or four times a week and she never mentions my transition—not a word. I write something in every mail, some little detail... how I feel, the changes I'm seeing, how my voice is dropping... something. She never responds. Just tells me about the weather, the dog, what she's doing in the yard. She does respond when I write about being lonely. Tells me she's lonely, too." I shook myself and reached for my wallet. "I'll get

34

this one." Marla opened her mouth to protest, but I handed the tab and my credit card to the server who was passing by. "Next time." The smile came more easily now, in spite of the hurt.

"So, are you going say anything to her?" Marla asked when we'd sat a few moments longer.

"Probably not. She's frightened for me, for my marriage to Leah, what Leah's going through and for what people will think. She needs to see that I'm not going to turn in to some kind of monster. She needs to see people accept me for who I am, whether they understand or not. Right now all she can see is the daughter she's always known. She may never see anything else. All I can do is be patient. I've never been what she expected, but she's always forgiven my shortcomings and loved me for who I am." I poured the last drops of tea into my cup. The server returned my card and I signed the tag. We shrugged into our jackets and made our way out of the quiet restaurant.

Driving home I thought a long time about my mom. I had to admit, it hurt that she seemed to be ignoring my transition. My mother and I had been at odds most of my life. Long before my teen years and long after them. At four I had insisted, loudly, I was not like my sisters but, rather, a boy. Summer days, I'd pulled off my shirt and stuffed a rubber ball into my underpants to be just like the other boys in the neighborhood. I'd persisted well into my school years until I had been shamed and punished to a point I understood, at last, that what I knew about myself was not as important as what others told me about myself. Not until my forties had Mom and I made peace with one another. Still, deep in my heart, I'd held on to the certain knowledge of who I was, no matter how deeply I kept it hidden. But now I was acting upon it.

In the last four months I'd overcome much of the initial disquiet felt by some around me. The owner of the fabric store where I taught had worried that the ladies wouldn't accept me as an instructor—that longtime customers would be unable to accept the change, and that newcomers would be unwilling to accept a man teaching sewing. She'd asked me to "soft-pedal" it, to not discuss the obvious. I didn't promise, but I did agree not to be the one to bring it up.

On hormones for weeks, my voice was dropping rapidly into a male range. A workshop was scheduled that brought in many of the long-time customers, some of whom hadn't been in for some time. I walked into the gathering to hellos and comments on the thirty-some pounds I'd lost over the past few months. I returned the greetings and made my way to a seat. One of my favorite students, a woman of my mother's age or better, spoke up as I reached the empty chair beside hers.

"Oh, listen to your voice! Is your asthma acting up?" She caught my hand and looked up at me.

"No, Rosemary, I'm fine. I haven't seen you in a while. This is how my voice sounds all the time these days."

"Why on earth…" Her brows furrowed and she caught my hand, looking into my face. "You've lost weight. Are you sure you're alright?" She was standing now, looking me up and down, reminding me of my favorite great aunt, many years gone. I swallowed hard.

"Yes, I'm fine. In fact, I'm wonderful. I've been taking hormones for a while now, and I've changed my name to Owen." Her eyes got wide and a troubled look crossed her sweet face.

"You aren't going to stop teaching us to sew, are you?" she asked, her hand on my arm. I began to chuckle.

"Oh, Rosemary, I can't imagine not being here to teach you ladies to sew. I'd miss you much too much."

"Well then, in that case, I'm happy for you. You look very handsome." She threw her arms around me in a hug and I thanked her with a hug back.

Part IV

I sat, staring at the monitor, heels of hands resting on the edge of the keyboard as I read the email from my mother. Brief, as always, about the dog, the weather, the roses in the yard. No mention of my announcement that I was scheduled for surgery in just over three months. No mention of my deepening voice and the phone call I'd made to her that morning… the one she'd answered with a suspicious, "Who is this?" when I greeted her with my standard, "Hi, Mom…" Only my father had wanted a son. Her dream had been of a blue-eyed, blonde baby girl. I pulled in a deep breath and began to type.

Hi Mom—

Good to hear you are keeping busy. So am I. It's only three weeks until Leah gets home. I'm anxious to see her and happy that things are going well back in her old hometown. I'll be so glad when she can come home to stay, but family is important and we can't both be there, no matter how big the crisis.

I'm staying busy, feeding the animals and getting ready to go to San Francisco for my surgery. Have all my clothes ready to pack. Leah and I are going a couple of days early, just to spend some time together before I am laid up for six weeks. I know it's going to be hard on her, coming home after so long with her friend Catherine and everything they've gone through this year with the cancer.

I'm sure they are both appalled at my timing, my insistence that I have what must seem to them to be the exact same surgery (by choice) when Catherine has felt so robbed in having to give up her breasts to cancer. I don't know that I'll ever be able to explain to them, or anyone, how different it is for me. What a relief it will be to separate myself from these mountains of flesh! It has taken a long time to convince Leah that my wanting them gone is about me, not about her, or about breasts in general. I love her, and I love women, I just wasn't meant to be one.

I don't know how to explain to you, either, that it's not anything you did, not anything dad did with his cruelty, or his using me for his own gratification when I was young. It has nothing to do with anything outside of me, but what came from within that made me know, deep inside, that I was always meant to be male.

Do you remember that time, when I was eight, and we were driving down Main Street in Woodland, past the Elks hall on Third Street? We were in the old red station wagon and I was hanging over the front seat. I saw that woman on the corner. She was dressed in a man's tweed suit, with a fedora on her silver haired head, leaning on a walking stick. She looked regal to me. I pointed to her and said,

"Look, Mom! I'm going to look like that someday!" You smacked me, hard, and I landed on the back seat. It's alright. I understand, now, what was happening. You were doing your best with what you knew. Had you heard of Christine Jorgenson, then? Did it flash in your mind that someday I might do what she had done, but in reverse? Did such things even enter your mind? I didn't think of it again until well into high school, but by then I'd resigned myself to the assumption that it couldn't be done, so I didn't talk about it anymore.

Mom, I love you. I know you love me, too. You've stuck with me through so much in my life, I know you'll find a way to accept my decision and trust I'm doing what I need to do. I hope you'll think about coming out to visit this summer. There are sewing workshops planned for June and I want you to be there with me.

Well, looks like this has turned into another one of those letters. I'm lonely and needing to feel some connection with the people who mean the most to me in my life, so I'm going to send this message even though it may make us both a little uncomfortable.

Love, Owen

Part V

It was March 15th. Leah's plane was due at eleven. The house was clean, my shirts ironed, and I was ready to make the drive to the airport. I sat at the computer, endlessly checking the email, killing time. The television was on to fill up the emptiness. It was nearly time to leave, but no use going too early only to circle the airport like a hungry shark, burning fuel. I tapped the key again, watching to see if anything would land in my inbox. Something did.

38

Hi—

It rained like crazy last night, too. I checked the rain gauge and we had over an inch. It was beautiful today and we had sunshine all day. No leaks down the wall out on the rug.

Your Aunt Marge is coming down and staying at Ann's since I don't have a bed. She is going to the Cancer Center on Wednesday to see a specialist, so we will see what the outcome is. I really feel sorry for her, having watched what they go through. We are all having dinner together and planning on playing a few games that evening.

When is your surgery scheduled? It's going to take a while for you to be able to do anything like even driving. I hope Leah stays awhile.

Nothing else to write about. So I'll close.

Love, Mom

I read the letter again. At last, after seven months, those two lines mentioning the surgery were the blessing I had been waiting for. It would take a while, but she'd come around. I hit the reply button and began to type.

Hi Mom—

Glad the rug is staying dry. I guess the cost of replacing the window was worth it. Now you can get the rug replaced and it'll all be good.

Looks like Wednesday is a big one, all around. My surgery is at 7:30 in the morning. I'm first in. Beats having to hang out half the day, waiting for my turn, starving because I can't have food or water. I can go a long time without either, but not once someone tells me "No, you can't." Surgery is supposed to take about two hours, so Leah should know how I'm doing by about 10:30—earlier if the doctor is the kind who comes out and talks to family as soon as he's done. She'll call you when they let her know it's over. They'll wake me up and send me back to the hotel as soon as they can pour me into my clothes and be sure I can hold something down. I don't expect any trouble with it.

I hope Leah is going to be able to stay a while, too. It just depends on what is happening with Catherine—she's finished radiation so there shouldn't be a problem. I'll be able to drive in about five days, after the drains come out, but can't lift or carry anything for about a month. The boys will be here if I need them. We talked originally about Leah going back as soon as I could drive if Cath needed her, but I don't know, now that she's finished with treatment.

Well, the plane will be in soon. I need to go.

Love, Owen

Part VI

It was Easter. I'd been recovering for a month. Mom and I had talked on the phone the day after surgery. Since then we'd traded half a dozen emails or more, each week, mine telling her in detail about my progress, assuring her I was feeling very little discomfort and healing fast and well. Half a dozen times I'd asked her to make plans to come out to visit. Her emails had lapsed immediately back into her newsy briefs about my aunt, my nephew, my sister and her own daily doings, with no mention of my invitation. I found an Easter card in my inbox and started a thank-you email.

Hi Mom—

Happy Easter. I'm feeling really good and am looking to start a new project to burn some of the new energy I've got. Leah has taken an interest in quilting, so we ordered a kit and I'm going to help her get started. She wants to do it all by hand, so once I teach her about cutting and using a needle I'm stepping back. She's signed up for the hand quilting class next time it comes up. She's going to start on a traditional piece and see where that leads.

I'm recovering really well, getting back to all of my usual activities. Yesterday I had to unload hay and feed from the pickup. Curtis is on a tear right now, not coming home because we want him to work and go to school or we don't let him use the car. I had to get the horses fed, so I unloaded stuff myself, carefully, not lifting the hay bales, but rolling them off the truck into the hay box. Just had to push them around a little. I'm starting to lift light weights and do pushups again. Got lots of weight to lose.

Leah and I are doing really well these days. We are both happier than we have been in many, many years. We've been able to be much more honest with each other about how we feel. She finally understands why I've been so closed off for all these years. Having no more secrets has opened up the relationship. We are starting to go out and have some real fun, and to have people over to our house. Leah is getting to know and truly appreciate the friends I made while she was gone. We have them in for potlucks and go to ball games together. She has totally accepted me as Owen, and often calls me her husband, with a smile.

Mom, I know you're still really upset by my transition. I know you can't begin to understand why I've done it, but I also know you love me and want me happy. This truly has made me happy. I have absolutely no regrets about what I've done. I've lost nothing and gained what I've most needed—peace of mind. It's impossible to explain what it feels like to know the body I was given didn't fit the person I am. If you've never felt it, there's no frame of reference for it, except to imagine yourself walking around being mistaken for someone who looks just like you. People expect you to know things, and feel things, and do things the way that other person would do them. They call you by a name that doesn't feel right. They don't listen when you tell them they've made a mistake. Just because you look like that other person, they insist you are that other person. You start to feel like you don't matter. They tell you you're crazy, but you know you're not—you're just not the person they think you are. Proving it seems impossible.

My friends and even my kids see how different I am these days. How relaxed and happy and settled I am. I don't get upset anymore when a stranger mistakes me for that other person, unless they're rude or nasty about it. One of the funniest things I've noticed about myself these days is that I've totally stopped biting my nails. Totally. They aren't soft and flexible any more, but hard and growing out to the tips of my fingers for the very first time. I know it's a silly thing to be excited about, but I've always seen them as an indicator of my stress level. I've never felt so good. I finally feel like a whole, real person.

Judy's doing a one-day sewing workshop June 11th at the hotel where we did our three-day retreat last year. I really want you to come and stay a week and go to it with me. I'll drive up and get you so you don't have to drive. Or, if you do want to drive, you can be happy that the peacocks are all gone and won't walk on your car. We don't miss them.

Love, Owen

Two hours later another email appeared in my inbox with the usual chit-chat about church, the dog's teeth, the neighbors. Then, near the end…

I want you to know I'm not upset about your change. It's not easy getting along in this world and being comfortable. I understand because I'm not all that comfortable either and hate trying to fit in.

42

I'd rather just stay home and not have to think about it. I really love you and want whatever makes you happy.

Love, Mom

P. S. I tried to send Leah a card but I'm not sure if I got the right address.

The screen blurred for a moment. In five lines my mother had just confirmed how very deeply connected we are. The unconditional love I had counted on was there. So was the shyness and discomfort we had both lived with throughout our lives. She trusted me to make choices that would be right for me, she was proud of me for doing what I could to make myself comfortable in this world.

Hi Mom—

Thank you. I don't know if you realize how much I needed to hear that from you. We were so far apart for so many years. I've treasured the last six years and how much closer we've become. I don't want to lose that. Life is too short and we missed out on a lot. I want the years left ahead of us to be good.

Start planning to come, and stay as long as you want. The weather should be great and you'll enjoy being here and seeing how happily things are going with us. No more petty gripes and misunderstandings. The cloud has lifted and life is good. I'm excited to have our lives running in parallel again.

Got to run now.

Love, Owen

Part VII

Mom called at noon from the bottom of the hill. She hates our mountain road, so we always meet her there and I drive her sporty red car up the twisting road to our house. Leah dropped me at the corner and went to town to shop for groceries. Mom was waiting in the passenger seat, her dog, Sassy, in her lap. I slipped into the driver's seat.

"I made it, and only took one detour." Her voice was bright and she laughed. It was our running joke that she drove a different route every time she came.

"You do better all the time. I'm proud of you. One of these days you'll start getting bored with doing it the same every time." I took the winding road slowly, knowing how she loathed the curves and the climb, even as she enjoyed the forest we traversed. The talk flowed comfortably between us. I relaxed into the seat, into the visit.

The house wasn't spotless, but it looked good for what it is. The furniture is sturdy and utilitarian. The big space in the middle of the library, our main room, held a table with a sewing machine and quilting tools. I laughed about turning the whole house into a studio for our art projects. We settled on the small sofa near the windows and talked. She told me about my aunt, my sisters, and all the goings on in the little town where I'd been born. Some part of me marveled at the easy tone we shared. There were still issues to settle, but we were there, together, and she was willing to face them with me.

Leah came in with a smile and hugs for Mom and me. I left them together and went out to unload the car.

Mom was in the guest room, turning down her bed and talking to Sassy. I padded down the hallway, headed to the bathroom, barefoot and shirtless. I'd shown her my scars that afternoon. She's a realist, taking life as it comes without much complaint. I'd heard no recrimination in her voice as she mentioned the dark hair growing on my chest where none had been before. She smiled and mused my father would have been jealous. She looked up as I neared her door.

"Sassy should be fine here in my room while we're at the workshop tomorrow," she said absently.

"Yeah, she does great when she's here. Leah will take her out and let her play." Smiling, I leaned my shoulder against the door jamb, watching

44

the dog sniff the carpet, wishing there was an easy way to say what was on my mind. It had been nearly a year since she had been with us last. The memory of that last workshop had preyed on my mind. Tomorrow was a chance to make a fresh start. We had already been to the fabric shop, seeing several of the women who had asked about her during the year. She was both embarrassed and pleased with the welcomes they gave her. They, and I, had politely overlooked her references to me as "she" that morning, some of them occasionally slipping themselves.

"There are going to be a lot of women there I don't know tomorrow." I felt awkward for the first time since her arrival. I forced myself to look at her, to hold my gaze level as she looked about the room. "They're going to see me as a man. Most of them will never think to question it. I really need for you to try hard not to out me. I don't expect you to call me Owen. I'd really like it, but I do understand how hard it is. But I do need you to realize how embarrassing it could be for everyone concerned, including you, if you refer to me as "she." The way I look now, they're going to think you're a little nuts if you refer to me as female." I smiled, trying to lighten the tension in the room. She stopped refolding the clothes in the top of her suitcase.

"I don't do it to be mean," she said with a shrug, the discomfort straining her voice. "I've called you my daughter for fifty years. I just don't think."

"You've got to think, Mom," I breathed, genuinely sorry for her in that moment. "You've got to. Not thinking could get me hurt… seriously hurt. In some places it could get me killed." She met my eyes at last, torn. I took a deep breath. "If we are out somewhere, and some guy overhears you calling me 'she' as I walk into the men's room, he could decide to express his objection to my gender and beat the living hell out of me."

"Well, you *don't* use men's rooms… do you?" Her voice trailed off so I barely heard the last words.

"Yes, Mom, I certainly do. My driver's license identifies me as male. My legal name is Owen. If I walked into a women's restroom and someone called security, the cops would haul me out, take one look at my ID and toss me into a patrol car in handcuffs. Most of them would not be kind. Some of them would be worse when they found out the bottom line truth." She flinched. I hated the images I had put in her head, but she could no longer ignore the truth, no matter how she tried to insulate herself from the harsh realities of the world. She met my eyes. "As long as I don't draw attention to myself I'm perfectly safe," I said softly, with a sad little smile. "Sleep well, Mom. I'll see you in the morning."

The morning was cool and cloudy. The coffee was good and so was the presentation. At the break I left the meeting room and headed for the public men's room in the lobby of the small hotel. I chuckled that the good thing about being the only man in a gathering of sixty was that I'd not have to wait in line. As I rounded the corner… I stopped short. There were two lines of women, one in front of each of the doors.

"We've commandeered your restroom," one of the women giggled nervously. I smiled and held my hands up in a gesture of surrender. "We'll give it back as soon as the ones in there are finished."

"No, no, just carry on. I'll wait my turn until after you're all done." One of the women, a student in past classes, smiled at me with a twinkle in her eye. I stood there, stifling a laugh, letting them take my silence for unease or good manners.

The line soon dispersed and I hurried back downstairs. Mom looked at me oddly, asking what had taken me so long. I smiled. "There was a line."

Age 43   Age 66

Robyn Walters is a 73-year-old post-op MTF from Maui whose husband is FTM. She still supports U.S. Navy ship maintenance projects part-time and uses that pay for family travel and the Maui mortgage.

A Journey from Young Boy to Old Woman

We shared several things, my father and I. He was an engineer; I was an engineer. He married and had a child; I married and had children. He had a love of science and instilled that love in me as well.

There were some glaring differences, though. He didn't stop smoking until it was too late, succumbing to lung cancer at age 56. I stopped smoking 30 years ago and have celebrated my 73rd birthday. He was a man. I appeared to be a man, but, to me, it felt like a charade.

I sometimes wonder if my father could have had a greater impact on my masculinity. The answer seems to be no. He could not have strengthened something that was just plain foreign to me. Perhaps I was ultimately better off for not having been forced to assume macho images

47

my father might have preferred to see in me but never imposed. I think my high level of inner turmoil was made more bearable by not being challenged.

My mother had more impact on me than my father. During my early years, she was nurturing, protective, and fun. She seemed not to mind that I was a quiet boy, not given to the boisterous actions of my peers. She never insisted that I go out into the rough and tumble life of the neighborhood toughies. I did, at times, but without a lot of success, and I much preferred books for companionship.

Baseball was okay. Sandlot baseball with elementary school friends was fun. We played in a big lot across from the train station in Madison, NJ. I even hit a home run once.

When that lot was paved and turned into commuter parking the next year, my halcyon baseball days were over. Instead, it was summer programs at the YMCA with pure torture in the gym and the swimming pool. I was the small one, the weak one. I was the one made fun of during the swim periods. Oh, how I hated to expose my underdeveloped body in the midst of boys who were beginning to look and act like men. "Hey, kid, are you ever going to grow any hair?"

If swimming and diving off the three-meter tower were bad, the pommel horse and rope climb were worse. Lack of coordination and upper body strength left me stuck halfway and feeling very inadequate. Why couldn't I be a successful, sweaty boy like the others?

The answer might have been apparent had someone seen this incident when I was nine. I had wandered into my parents' closet after school one day and wiggled my way into one of my mother's dresses. I don't recall what it looked like, but I remember a silky lining and a wonderful fragrance. Panicky, I hung the dress back up and ran out of the room, forgetting one detail.

"Bobby," my mother called when she came home from work, "the light is on in my closet. Did you go in there for something?" Lying was never my strong suit, but inspiration saved me that day. "Um, yes Mom. You said I could use your roller skates, and I was skating in the kitchen for a while."

Phew. I had survived my first cross-dressing experience. To be nearly caught, however, had been terrifying.

Years passed and my body began to mature, sort of. There were strange sensations and urgings that no one told me to expect. One day, when I was twelve, I tried on my mother's wedding gown, but it was many sizes too big for a scrawny boy. I didn't think to look in a mirror, which was probably a blessing. As I folded the velvet gown and went to put it back, I noticed a beautiful lace-trimmed rayon chemise that had been left under the gown. Flesh colored and incredibly silky, that garment released many of the physical sensations that come to pubescent lads. Soon I designated it as mine and moved it to a safe spot in my bedroom, the first in a collection that spanned decades.

I remember visiting backyard clotheslines at age 13 or 14 while walking home at night from Catechism classes. There are also memories of poking through the laundry basket at a cousin's house. It wasn't long before I actually started wearing lingerie.

In my sophomore year, I walked uptown with a friend. He explained that he was too busy and had to give up his after-school job. I jumped at the opportunity. My parents were surprised when I announced at dinner that I had a part-time job in our town's photo shop. I learned a lot from the owner. Working with the public also gave me a lot of poise. Adults were easier to deal with than macho boy classmates or the girls I liked but didn't know how to behave around. Occasionally, there were days when I handled the store all by myself. Sometimes I "underdressed" while there. The feel of a slip next to my skin was both comforting and exciting.

The greatest pleasures of my high school days were my job, my studies, and flying model airplanes. My airplanes weren't as good as those of my two close buddies, and I wasn't as skilled as they were at making them do loops. But, it was fun. And it instilled in me a dream to really fly someday. During those years I also began a lifelong amateur radio hobby.

High school academics weren't particularly difficult. I was surprised to end up valedictorian of my class. I enjoyed being the lighting director for several plays and talent shows. Learning the current state of the art lighting system was fun, and I enjoyed mixing and matching the colors. Lavender was my favorite. And I especially loved watching the girls onstage in their pretty gowns.

My high school days weren't without challenge. I was still far different from most of the boys in my class. They seemed interested only in cars, cigarettes, beer, and sex. I didn't know or care too much about any of those delights.

Girls were a disaster. I was attracted to some of the girls and to their clothes. But I didn't know how to relate to girls and rarely had a date. I do have some pictures of girls in braces and pretty gowns with this gawky kid (me) in an ugly suit and bow tie. One girl wore a white satiny scoop-neck gown I would have given my eyeteeth for. Oh well, at least I had my lingerie stash. I discovered that a lingerie love life was always available and quite satisfying. Too inept to have a girlfriend, I still managed to keep the pubescent male machinery well-exercised.

Late in my senior year, I found my first real girlfriend. Estelle and I spent a lot of time together, convinced that we were in love forever. We shared a lot of fumbly excitement, but I managed to avoid intercourse. First of all, as a good young Catholic, I wasn't supposed to, and second, I didn't have a clue as to how to do it.

Estelle and I lasted not quite a year. We broke up in the spring of my freshman year of college. My heart was broken, but I was still living at home with access to my lingerie stash. And there was studying to do.

In June 1956, a skinny kid rode from Jersey south to Annapolis, Maryland with his parents. The sun was shining when we stopped at a lookout on the approach to the Severn River Bridge. The Naval Academy was just off to the left on the far side of the river, with Chesapeake Bay spreading out behind its seawall. Breathtaking. It was to be my home for the next four years.

Gone was any thought of privacy. Gone—for a short time—was any doubt of masculinity. Hey, I was a Midshipman, the cream of the crop. I was going to be an Admiral. But the other guys—most of them—were so macho and so much stronger than I. There were some who didn't care for this bookish, non-athletic kid from New Jersey. But I had a good roommate for all four years, and I not only had the advantage of being a good student but also that of having already had freshman engineering. I finished Plebe Year with only ten demerits out of 600 allowable and a 3.9 academic average out of 4.0.

Hours after the Naval Academy class of 1957 graduated and threw their hats in the air, close to 500 of my classmates and I were shuttled to an armada of ships standing in Chesapeake Bay. The other half of my class went home for six weeks of summer leave.

And what a ship my first ship was—the USS Iowa, lead ship in the last and largest class of battleships in the US Navy. It was huge, massive, and with 16-inch guns that could throw a projectile the weight of a Volkswagen Beetle 20 miles. I learned how to holystone the teak fantail under the watchful eye of a first class Bosun's Mate.

In Rio de Janeiro I got laid. First time. Second and third time, too. Now I was a man. I proudly took my penicillin pill each night when I came back to the ship to prevent venereal disease. It was an experience of a lifetime. When I was home on leave I was very frustrated. No woman to seduce, no young Brazilian prostitutes to pay, and I had thrown my lingerie stash away when I left for the Academy.

Back to the Naval Academy in late August, no longer a plebe. Now I was a "Youngster" and had some privileges, among them the right to date. By the time that year was over I had had several dating experiences and an honest-to-goodness girlfriend. We were married after graduation.

In June 1960, I was commissioned an ensign in the US Navy, and my wife and I settled into an apartment in Washington, DC. We soon had a baby on the way, and I was working 5½ days a week designing nuclear submarine fluid systems. Pretty good, except that I didn't have a clue how to be a husband or a father. I did better on the father side than on the husband side and our marriage was soon on a downhill slide. I started another lingerie stash that was kept in a paper bag atop a ventilation duct in the basement of the townhouse where our second daughter was conceived.

There wasn't a lot of socializing at work. The admiral frowned on anything that wasn't work related. At the few gatherings we did have, the husbands and wives were segregated, and I had to endure stories about work when I would have been more comfortable in the women's circle.

After four years I received orders to the guided missile cruiser USS Little Rock. We moved to Norfolk, but the lingerie stash stayed behind. To this day, I wonder if it's still hidden there above the vent duct. There was little opportunity to replenish my stash while there, although I did manage to hide a few small items in the stateroom I shared with another officer. Eventually, I threw them overboard in the Mediterranean Sea. I now know this is a typical pattern for cross-dressers called "purging."

Following that sea tour the Navy sent me to MIT for naval engineering graduate studies. We owned a house, and it had a perfect hidey-hole in the downstairs bathroom which eventually held two bags of lingerie. I began to wear lingerie whenever my family was away.

We were in the seventh year of our, by now, loveless marriage. One night, in my frustration, I took a beautiful nightgown from my wife's dresser; one that she never wore. I accidentally fell asleep with the nightgown spread on top of me. My wife never said a word, but the cat was sneaking out of the bag. I put the nightgown away when I awoke the next morning and stayed away from her things for some time.

When we divorced, several years later, she stayed in the house. So far as I know, the house was sold with those two bags of lingerie still hidden in the bathroom ceiling.

That summer, I met a woman in a physics class I was teaching after my daytime Navy job. I was waiting for my divorce to be final. Nicky was separated from her husband. By late fall she was living with me, and I felt like a man again. A year later Nicky and I married and were very quickly in a family way. In Brunswick, Maine, sixteen months apart, our two daughters were born.

To my surprise, I had enough oomph and XY chromosomes to father four daughters, two of whom have given birth to six daughters of their own.

Life settled into a comfortable pattern of Navy, work, family, and hobbies. I spent many hours improving my flying skills. And I was able to put up some decent antennas for my amateur radio station. But always in the background were the lingerie stashes and the occasional opportunity to try on a skirt and blouse from my wife's side of the closet.

The radio room was downstairs and held a desk, two computers, and several radios. Adjoining the room was a bathroom with shower. As a considerate husband I shaved and showered there in the early morning hours so as not to disturb my wife. The morning routine involved changing from pajamas to a nightgown and then back again, before returning upstairs to eat and dress for work. I'd lie on the floor doing stretching exercises and could almost feel the breasts that should have been there. Most mornings there was a sexual tension that had to be released as well.

Eventually I yielded to the pressure from my wife and started an account with an Internet Service Provider. We were on the World Wide Web! Well, I was. Nicky very quickly lost interest in it. One day I typed "cross-dresser" into the Yahoo search engine, and my world changed. I found out that I wasn't alone.

Several years later, I told Nicky I was a cross-dresser. She informed me that our marriage was over. I was crushed. She had so many gay and lesbian friends; how could she not accept me as a cross-dresser and end our marriage? Easy; she thought it perverse. She felt betrayed. Her femininity was threatened.

She said, "Why didn't you tell me 23 years ago, before we married? How can I trust you? What if I trusted you and you later decided to change your sex?"

"Oh my God. Change sex? No, no, I'm just a cross-dresser. That's all I want to be."

"I don't think so," she replied, bitterly. "When you retire next year— without me—you will be living full-time as a woman in no time."

How absurd, I thought. I just want to be able to wear a dress now and then, buy a wig, and go to the mall as Robyn, my feminine self. Nothing more. I'm just a cross-dresser. That's what was behind my almost 50 years of lingerie fetish. Well, there was also the fantasy of having breasts, but, no, I'm just a cross-dresser.

She was wrong. I didn't go full-time immediately. No, I waited for nine months. Sheesh! I guess she understood it better than I.

I missed the 1997 alternative community Halloween party by a day when I arrived on the West Coast to begin my retirement. The boxes of women's clothes and my wig remained in the trunk of my car until I moved into my new house. "Robyn" then remained in the lingerie drawer until Easter 1998. That morning she introduced herself at church, wearing a lilac suit, a cloyingly sweet old lady blouse, a pretty corsage, and too much makeup. I knew better than to try heels. Reaction was mixed, but overall supportive.

A month later came an event that changed my life. Esprit is the Pacific Northwest Gender Conference, and it was less than a hundred miles away. Robyn went.

Five days as me, the real me! I felt liberated, validated, even though I wasn't as nicely dressed as many of the other cross-dressers, nor did I have breasts like some I noticed. Breasts, real breasts.

I should have gone to the meeting about how to cope with Blue Monday, the first Monday after the conference when we all return to our regular lives and the girl clothes are hidden away and no longer worn. So when I arrived home, I drove right up my neighbors' driveway to pick up my mail and said, "Hi, time to let you know that I'm a cross-dresser." Neighborhood reaction was mixed, but mostly unsupportive.

So there I was, out in the neighborhood and pretty much shunned. I began gender counseling so as to better understand this drive to live like a woman.

Between cross-country trips to see my wife, my therapist had a heart-to-heart talk with me.

"Robyn," she said, "I have good news and bad news."

"Oh? What's the good news?"

"The good news is that you aren't a cross-dresser."

"Hey. All right! Maybe I can save my marriage after all. Um. What's the bad news?"

"The bad news is that you are a transsexual. What are you going to do about it?"

"My God," I asked, "how did you come up with that?"

"You told me," she replied. "You said you'd like to live as a woman and that you'd like a feminine body."

It seems that cross-dressers don't want to change their bodies and don't want to live full-time as a woman. They happily put away the weekend girly things and easily step back into the male role. I dreamed of breasts and felt I could be happier living as a woman than living as the man I had tried so hard to be. The therapist was right; I was a transsexual.

Still, I went back to the East Coast several times, trying to save my marriage. No joy. On my last visit, my wife asked what she'd find if she did come out for a visit. I told her that I was living full-time as Robyn. She cried when she dropped me off at the airport for the last time.

Events began to unfold in rapid manner. In September 1998, I pierced my ears, telling the young lady at the mall that I had just gotten my mother's permission at age 61.

"Nice," said my therapist. "You may be full-time, but your 'Real Life Experience' doesn't begin until you've changed your name." The Real Life Experience, a minimum one-year period spent living in one's new gender role, is required before authorization is given for sex reassignment surgery. My doctor wouldn't start the clock until I legally became Robyn.

On the 8th of October, I stood before the judge in a half-filled courtroom. I wore a long skirt and blouse. My hair was better, and so was my makeup. I was sworn in and answered the judge's questions. "No, your honor, I'm not changing my name for any fraudulent or illegal reasons."

He signed the petition with a flourish, and said, "Your name is now Robyn Marie. Enjoy your new name, sir."

I flushed with anger at being called "sir"—I had voted for the sonofabitch—but I kept my cool and turned to walk out. A gentleman—a real gentleman—three rows back, smiled and sent me a high five.

My therapist wrote a letter authorizing hormonal reassignment. I took my first Premarin tablet on the first of December. No stopping me now. I'm a woman. I always was a woman, but now it will be right.

Women friends were different, now. They told me things that made my jaw drop. I realized that women are very open and intimate among themselves. Sure wasn't like guy talk. I loved the openness; I loved the trust; I loved the belonging; and I learned—a lot.

But no surgery. I was a non-op transsexual woman. I didn't need surgery to be a woman. My therapist told me so. I was happy with myself just as I was, until one day in February 1999 while exercising my Navy retirement benefit of shopping at the submarine base grocery store.

Three base policemen walked in and spoke briefly with the manager. Hmmm, I thought, there must be some shoplifting going on. One of them walked straight up to *me*. There was no "hello," no "please." Just, "You have to come outside with me—now. Leave your shopping cart."

"Walk over to the squad car."

"Show me your identification."

I had practiced this scene. I think all transgendered people do. I calmly produced my driver's license, which was marked female.

"Let me see your Department of Defense ID."

I showed the policeman my retired Navy ID card, which had been changed only the week before to reflect my new legal name. Navy ID cards do not show gender.

"We had a complaint by a store employee that a transvestite used the ladies room."

"I'm not a transvestite," I replied to the policeman, who was half my age or less. "I am a transsexual. Would you like to see my diagnosis letter?"

"No, that's okay. Have you had surgery?"

"Not yet, officer. There is a requirement for transsexuals to live in their new gender for at least one year before they can be authorized for sex reassignment surgery."

"Well," he said, shaking his head, "we would have gotten the same call if you had used the men's room."

"I'm not allowed to use the men's room, anymore."

His compatriots came out of the commissary. They all moved off to the side and conversed.

My policeman came back and said, "The two women who complained weren't actually in the ladies room. They just remembered seeing you as a man when you first used the commissary over a year ago. We have to call our sergeant and see if we should bring you down to the station."

He left again and the three of them radioed their sergeant. When he returned, he said, "The sergeant said to let you go. I'm sorry we had to bother you."

"That's okay," I said. "You did what you had to do, and I appreciate that you were such a gentleman."

My knees were shaking but I marched back into the commissary, showing both my Navy ID and my female driver's license, and went straight to the manager's office. He was embarrassed and apologized profusely. When I went back to get my cart the two women scowled at me. I just smiled at them. Everyone else was friendly and supportive.

I didn't see the scowling employees after that, but the damage had been done. I realized that there was a sword hanging over my head. I could be stopped by any security guard or policeman and subjected to questioning or worse. I might be able to go to a ladies restroom but never to a ladies locker room. I could never go to a swimming pool. I'd always be looking over my shoulder. That realization made me think long and hard. A week later, I made an appointment to see a sex-reassignment surgeon, Dr. Toby Meltzer, then in Portland, Oregon.

In April 1999 the surgeon evaluated my body, took my $500 deposit, and gave me a surgery date for October 2000. The date moved up a few months, and I actually had my surgery on my 63rd birthday in June 2000.

So my father's son became a woman, and my husband was there when I awoke.

Oh, yes. That is part of my journey, too. Shortly after I had my interesting discussion with the young policeman I met a wonderful man on an online news list for transgender elders. We came to have very strong feelings about each other, falling in love in cyberspace. In September 1999 I flew to Michigan to meet him and his family. After ten days we parted company an engaged couple. I began divorce proceedings when I arrived home. In November, Emery arrived, ready to begin the test; if we could still love each other after a rainy Pacific Northwest winter, we would marry.

And we did. We married on Valentine's Day 2000, about four months before my surgery. Legally married, as in one male, one female. On our marriage documents, Robyn was listed as male and Emery as female. That's the way it was on that day. Today, I am female and my husband is male. He is a Meltzer alumnus, too, having undergone female-to-male reassignment surgery,

Unusual, perhaps, and fairly rare. If the odds of being transsexual are one in 10,000, then the odds of husband and wife both being transsexuals should be about one in 100,000,000, meaning about three such couples in America. However, we have already met five or six MTF/FTM couples, so the odds are better than they might seem; and why not? Who can understand a transsexual partner better than another transsexual?

So here we are, an older transsexual couple with kids, grandkids, three cars, a house, a condo, and a mortgage. Is our journey over? No way. Is our journey good? You bet.

What next? Well, there is a lot of civil rights work that needs to be done before transgendered people can live free of legal discrimination. As a board member of the PFLAG Transgender Network, I am playing an active part in the struggle. It's what keeps me young. That and working full-time for several months each year when the Navy asks my company to bring me back to help out.

Age 22   Age 37

Christopher Robin is a poet from Santa Cruz, California. His interests include poetry, making zines, traveling, and playing online pool. He is the co-host of a weekly poetry reading in a laundromat and has written three chapbooks of poetry, his latest is entitled Angelflies in My IdiotSoup.

A Nonconformist

One of my earliest memories was asking my mother, while sitting on her lap, if I could be turned into a boy. She said of course not, that she loved her little girl. But I didn't want to be a little girl, and I continued to run around the yard without a shirt on, playing rough, riding my bike, skateboarding, and teasing the girls.

As I got older, I actually believed I was a boy. My grandmother lived in the mountains of Nevada. In the summertime, I roamed around the creeks, collecting arrowheads and fishing with the dog—until I was shamed by socialization, that is.

I don't know why I decided to learn to curl my hair and wear makeup when I was around 13 years of age, but I tried. There was quite a bit of pressure from my friends and older sister, I gather. I also remember some of the boys telling me I should act "more like a girl." I tried it for a few years but became somewhat of a rebellious tomboy instead, eventually evolving into a teenage-punk-rock-nonconformist and political activist. As the years went on, my many incarnations were to include: femme lesbian, bisexual alcoholic, gender-non-specific-gypsy-clown, heterosexual carnie, and Dianic Witch (not in that order). Looking back, I consider all of these roles essential on my road to becoming a whole human being. I don't regret nor discount any of them.

But the more I sobered up (in 1994 at age 24), the more masculine I started to feel. I started dressing more and more like a male, walking around my neighborhood in the River Flats defending women from unsavory men, and striving to become more sturdy and confident.

As the years went on I began to bind my breasts and to crave testosterone in what seemed to be a physiological way. My body and mind felt fragmented. I didn't feel whole or balanced in the way I was presenting. I wasn't a drag king or a butch. What was I? I didn't completely relate to the other butches I knew. They didn't want to grow facial hair and pass as men like I did. Eventually I realized I was transgendered. At the time I was surrounded by lesbians, most of them very anti-patriarchal, anti-male, and who could blame them? My mother, a feminist, asked me early on why I would ever want to become a man, as "men are smelly, rude and worthless." All true, I agreed, but I didn't have to become those things, I could become my own man. Nowadays I am my own man, but sadly, I am also those aforementioned things (to varying degrees) depending on what time of the day it is.

But I digress. I went to the FTM conference in Seattle in May of 2001 at age 31. I learned so many things, about passing, packing, sex, dating, but what I was really looking for was to learn about the medical aspects of taking testosterone, since I had been living with a brain injury since 1991. I was concerned that testosterone would make me more aggressive and prone to anger, as I was already prone to those things due to my brain injury. At the conference I met transpeople who also had disabilities and were leading full lives as their true selves, and I realized that it was possible for me as well. On the drive back to California, I knew I'd had a breakthrough.

I met my girlfriend, Jenny, in June of that year at a gay pride rally. She had recently begun her own hormone treatments to become a full-time woman (MTF). We took the journey together, including group therapy and weekly trips to San Francisco to the free clinic for our hormones and checkups. After a few months on T, my psychiatrist said my anger seemed to be subsiding, that the hormones were actually helping my mind become steadier, and he took me off all psychiatric drugs. (I had been on various psychiatric medications for ten years.) I haven't had to be on any medication since. And it's true: both my mental and physical energy improved, at least for the first few years of hormone treatment.

Jenny taught me a lot about being a man, and I scored some very expensive Italian suits (which had to be tailored of course). I went back in my biological memory as far as I could to help her become a woman, but I actually wasn't that helpful, much to her disappointment.

In 2004 I began the rigorous and exhausting process of finding a surgeon to perform my top surgery. I was tired of hiding myself, and I was very uncomfortable in my body. There had been a couple of Medi-Cal (low-income insurance) cases where transsexuals had their surgery covered under this plan. With the help of Jenny, skilled in both law and jumping through the flaming hoops of bureaucracy, and a helpful lawyer in San Francisco, we got Medi-Cal to agree to pay for my procedure under "medical necessity." But it wasn't that easy. Finding a surgeon who would accept the Medi-Cal proved to be a nightmare. The surgeon who had agreed to do it a year earlier retired just as I won my appeal. He was the only surgeon in California who would even consider such insurance, as historically Medi-Cal would either not pay the surgeons at all or the reimbursement would be too low to make it worth their while. It was time to take drastic measures.

Luckily, three years before I had received an unexpected settlement from Social Security, and had bought a big truck with the money (which fit in with my "macho" lifestyle at the time). I still had the truck. It was worth $5,000. Of course, $5,000 will not get you top surgery in California, no way no how. So I began to dig further until I found a kind surgeon in Oklahoma City who would perform the procedure in his office and let me stay in a nearby hotel for my recovery. It cost exactly what I got for my truck.

Accompanied by a friend who had some medical background, we checked ourselves into an Oklahoma City hotel near an abandoned go-kart track and a liquor store, and I continued with my journey into manhood. The surgeon's office was very clean and the staff extremely friendly. I don't remember the first few days. The pain was so bad it blocked out most of my memory, but there were no serious medical mishaps. If there had been, I may not have been able to check myself into the local hospital. I most likely would have been turned away.

I have never received the "male privilege" all the lesbians crowed about (all the while relieving me of my relationships with them, but not from the odd jobs they needed me to do in their yards). Perhaps there is some male privilege out there in the world, but for me, only when I take my car to the mechanic. There, they look at me instead of Jenny, as if I know what they're talking about. I don't. She does, but pretends not to.

So there is often this superficial assumption that because I present as a man, I must know something about *something*. The only thing I really know is how to pretend to understand them while they are talking, nod accordingly, and then give a "manswer." A "manswer" is a word my FTM buddy came up with. It is the made up "answer" when a male is asked a question and he doesn't know the answer. Considering my brain injury, I think I am the King of Manswers.

Nowadays my life is full of friends who accept me the way I am. Most of my friends are not transsexuals. I socialize with a variety of people of all persuasions: gay, straight, gender ambiguous, employed or hardly ever employed. My ideal when I began transitioning was not to surround myself solely with people from the trans community.

My current community is vast and covers a lot of territory. I participate in the larger world, not necessarily to assimilate, as that will never happen (being a transgendered, polyamorous, disabled poet, I am not exactly on the top of the food chain), but to embrace people of all types. As a writer, I cannot afford to paint myself into a corner, either culturally or sociologically. I need all different types of experiences and stimulating input. I have run a literary magazine since 2000 and get contributions from people all over the world. I also run a pen pal service for prisoners (many of them transgendered) and have published my poetry in many small magazines, as well as having been a featured reader around the country. With all this in mind, I will never label myself a transgendered writer, a queer writer, or even a disabled writer. I am a man of the world, yet a nonconformist to the bone, and always will be.

Allie Richards lives, works and thinks about gender in Wisconsin.

Musings on Gender and Hair

When I was perhaps eight years old my grandmother got me a pair of bright red corduroy pants; they quickly became my favorite and I wore them every chance I got. One day a boy yelled at me on the playground; he told me red pants were for girls. At the time it confused me, and I wondered why he'd say such a thing. After all they were my red pants, and I was a boy.

Today I am a feminist-minded queer woman, and my grandmother is no longer speaking to me. I suppose I should talk about what happened in between.

Not much stands out about growing up. I lived in a conservative family in the 1980's in the suburbs. I wasn't pressured to be other than the bookish kid I was. While this allowed me to not participate in typical boy behavior, there was still a definite boundary. I wasn't allowed to do things or participate in activities that were perceived as decidedly "girlish", e.g. dolls (although I never wanted any) were forbidden. But as long as I was just inside this boundary, things were fine.

My grandparents raised me, and I was very close to my grandmother when I was little. Because neither they nor my parents had friends with children, I was not around other children very much. I did a lot of reading, and my family went to church a minimum of three times a week. I went to a private school with the same core group of about 20 kids from preschool to 8th grade.

By the time I was in high school we were living in a smaller town, but I was going to a much larger school, as I was now in the public school system. It was a difficult adjustment and I couldn't wait to get out of there.

When I was in college I took some introductory philosophy courses from a professor I really liked. Later I noticed she was teaching a course in Women's Studies that fulfilled a requirement I needed and fit my schedule nicely. I was a bit apprehensive at the time because I didn't know anything about the subject other than the stereotypes about feminists that proliferated in rural communities like the one where I was living. But I already knew and liked the professor, so with a determination to keep an open mind I signed up for the class.

I struggled a lot in that class. The issues we talked about weren't nearly as immediate to me as to most of the people in the class, but as I listened to the discussion I started to grasp what was going on and I came away with a lot of important ideas. The one that really stuck with me was the concept of male privilege, which, loosely defined, can explain how and why sexism tends to be invisible to men. I started to realize that all of this gender stuff that everyone took for granted was a lot more complicated than it seemed. One of the articles we read was "Gender Quiz, Lunch, Profits" by Minnie Bruce Pratt. It included a small discussion of transgender issues within a broader context of queer issues. Most of it was over my head at the time, but I was fascinated by it. It touched on so many possibilities.

At the time I was concentrating on graduating, so it was a couple more years before I was able to revisit the things I had learned, but after getting out of school I began to do a lot of reading of feminist material on my own time. The ideas that resonated with me the most were those that touched on issues related to what gender is and how it works; I was learning about these issues and ideas while I was in the middle of struggling with how my own gender worked and how I related to it.

In 2000 I read *Manifesta: Young Women, Feminism and the Future* in which Jennifer Baumgardner and Amy Richards discussed a school of feminist thinking in which femininity is appreciated and valued rather than being rejected as being weak and vulnerable. With this idea in hand I realized I could transition without feeling disempowered.

So I got on the Internet, did a lot of research and quickly discovered that there was a very standard script that most transpeople followed (you've probably heard it before, it starts out with, "I've known since I was five years old..."). That wasn't a reflection of my experience or feelings, so I tried to just stop thinking about it. But it turned out that I couldn't just stop thinking about it, and since the existing discourse about transgender experiences didn't line up with mine, I realized I had to find my own way.

The best way to describe what I was feeling at the time is to say that I was obsessed about gender—my gender, other people's gender and how we come to know and understand ourselves as women or men. I asked a few of my friends at the time what their experience of their own gender was and got back responses like, "I don't really think about it" across the board. Since transitioning I'm a lot less obsessed with it too, which is probably one of the reasons why my views of gender are so much different today than they used to be.

Shortly before I transitioned, I wrote a letter to everybody in my family telling them what I was doing, and I gave them a bunch of information and several ways to contact me. I never heard anything back from anybody on my father's side of the family. I didn't hear from them to tell me I was going to hell. I didn't hear from them to tell me not to do it. I didn't hear from them that they were outraged, upset or disappointed. Nothing.

The other half of my family (my parents are divorced) does speak to me. I see them once or twice a year, usually around the holidays, which is about the same as it has always been.

My transition happened very quickly. It seemed long at the time. But it was just hormones and hair and… done. Hormones do some interesting things to you—they redistribute body fat, make your skin softer, you grow some breasts, whatever. Oh, and then you get your hair done, change your clothes, and that's it. Seriously, it's all about the hair, or at least it was for me. Here's how it happened: I made an appointment at a salon, walked in and said, "Hi, I'm on the cusp of a gender transition so I need a really girly haircut." The hairstylist just looked at me and said, "Sure, we'll do something cute, no problem." And that was it. I went into the salon looking male and I came out looking female.

The way I viewed the world and the way I thought about gender changed that afternoon. Immediately I experienced a drastic change in the way people related to me. I expected this, but I wasn't prepared for the intensity of it. People ignored my opinions and treated me like a child. I began to get catcalls and other forms of street harassment. I was expected to smile on demand, and by the way, my eyes are *up here*. Both my body and my actions were interpreted in vastly different ways than they were when I was perceived as male.

Another thing I noticed was all the messages designed to make women feel bad about themselves and about their bodies. I did not realize how hard that would hit me and again was not prepared for the intensity of it. Images of women in the media and the related pressures placed on women to be skinny and beautiful were suddenly things I was dealing with. I was already clued into feminism, which has helped a lot, but the messages still got to me.

I find men are more willing, now, to move or lift heavy things for me, which I actually like. I never had a lot of upper body strength to begin with and I lost a whole bunch after taking hormones. When people perceived me as male they would generally let me do heavy lifting on my own, even though they could see I was struggling. But now it's like, "No, no, no, don't get that, I'll get it." Okay, thank you.

It's not only other people that treat me differently, I'm acting somewhat differently now as well. I'm not doing it intentionally. There is a difference in how people treat me and how I think of myself, and it does, subtly or not so subtly, change how I act. Regardless, I'm expressing myself in ways that currently feel natural and comfortable to me. Before I transitioned I was much less comfortable with myself, so I tended to be very withdrawn. I'm still a bit shy, but am generally much more comfortable around people. Yet, I also notice that because of the expectations society places on women, I tend to be much less sure of myself.

I've found it really amazing how quickly those expectations come into play. To hear people talk about male socialization and female socialization you might think that socialization is this thing that happens to us right around puberty and then it's all over and you are socialized. But the truth is it's a constant and ongoing process, and a very potent one.

Because gender is socially constructed there really are only two options in terms of gender. When we interact with another person we each decide what gender the other person is and act accordingly; we have a binary gender system with fairly strict roles. Of course there are many other cues we use to figure out how to interact with other people, but gender tends to be the first and most important. Ultimately, I'd like to see the end of the binary gender system. I enjoy my gender, but there's no reason to think (as some people seem to) that the elimination of gender roles will cause the end of gender expression.

Most of the transpeople I've met view their gender identity as something that's predetermined, something they're born with. I think that's a popular view because it offers a possible explanation, at least to an extent, as to why someone would want to transition. I don't agree because I feel that that amounts to gender essentialism and I just can't get on board with that. Especially when looking at it from a civil rights perspective, saying that gender identity is a tiny piece of the brain we haven't yet discovered is a poor strategy, because transphobic (and homophobic) people aren't going to change their minds even if we could prove that gender identity (or sexual preference) is biological. Not to mention if something biological ever is discovered it might well be used as sort of a transgender (or gay) "litmus test" and may only serve to create division.

Just as I don't feel that my gender identity was necessarily predetermined, I don't feel like my sexual orientation was either (though I don't think that makes either of them any less real). I think of myself as queer (which, for me, means that I'm a woman who is primarily attracted to women, though I don't worry about it if I happen to become attracted to a man) but of course, as with most labels, it's not quite so simple.

I find (and this should come as a surprise to no one) that there is a lot of pressure placed on both men and women in our society to be straight. A lot of people seem to succumb to that pressure without ever questioning their sexuality much. When I was growing up I was expected to be straight, so I pretty much assumed I was. When I transitioned there was a whole new set of expectations, but there was still my memory and history. After a few very confusing months I started to be able to separate my own desires from the expectations placed on me. I started to realize that I could be attracted to people of any gender, but that I was more attracted to feminine people than to masculine people regardless of their gender. Some may say that makes me bisexual, but I don't like that term because it reifies the binary gender system. "Pansexual" is closer, but it still doesn't seem quite right, so I use "queer." I find that when I tell people I'm queer, even if I explain what I mean by it, they tend to assume I mean "lesbian," but I'm okay with that.

On the subject of labels, I don't usually use the terms "transgender" or "transsexual" to describe myself. It's true that I've gone through a gender transition, but it seems like such a very small part of who I am, so I'm content to let it be subsumed into "queer." I'm very out about being queer.

The question of why I changed my gender is one that I don't worry about much. I think people probably transition for a whole host of different reasons, and beyond that I don't think the "why" is very important. If someone wants to change genders, it doesn't matter why. Anyone should have the right to look and dress and live however they want. And how we get to the point of understanding ourselves is nobody's business. So I don't ask why. I express my gender in ways that feel comfortable to me and that's that. The only thing at all unique about me is that I went through a gender transition in order to do that.

And that is how a young boy with a penchant for bright colors grew up to be a queer woman with great hair.

Age 22   Age 28

Leon Mitchell was born 29 years ago to a Mexican woman and an American man. He's enamored of his Oaxacan roots and in awe of the American Dream. An artist by nature and a writer by solace, he is impassioned about life, art, and food. He works for a personal development organization as an artist and designer.

Transmutations

The sensation that there was something different about me began to haunt me when first I realized there was a difference between boys and girls. I was young enough to live in the present moment most of the time, but aware enough to understand other peoples' perception of me. One thing I knew for sure: something was not quite right. I knew it because everything coming from the outside was trying to convince me that I was a little girl, while everything within told me otherwise. Was it them? Or was it me?

In my earliest years the battle was not so much with myself as with other people. My mom told me not long ago that when I was about two or three years old whenever she would try to put a dress on me I would say, "No mom, can't you see I'm a boy? Look at me mom; look real good, because I'm a boy!" She thought it was just a cute phase. I have but a vague recollection of those moments but very clear memories of the annoyance I experienced throughout much of my early childhood. I found it silly of them to try to convince me that I was something other than who I was. Besides I was too busy pretending to be Batman, climbing trees and playing with action figures to really care. Every once in a while I was reprimanded for not acting "like a lady," but most of the time I was a happy tomboy. Yet I lived with the constant question: "Why can't you see who I really am?"

As I grew older I began to consider that perhaps everyone else was right and I was in the wrong. Perhaps there *was* something not right about me. How devastating those considerations turned out to be, for even though I could not find where I had gone wrong, I began to judge myself—and judgment begets punishment.

I vividly recall the confusion and sense of displacement that permeated my childhood and teenage years. As I look back, I can see myself becoming detached from myself. I stopped being Who I Am and surrendered to the pressure from the world. I learned to be someone I was not.

What was so wrong about wanting to play with the boys? Why was it improper to find no appeal in dolls, make-up and bows? Why was I yelled at for refusing to wear silly skirts? What was so wrong about being me?

I also remember the precious moments when I was "mistaken" for a boy or young man. Of course, to me there was no mistake—they were actually seeing me as I was! Looking back, I can see that these were invaluable moments of clarity and wellness for my True Being. Those brief encounters kept me from entirely losing my true self to the mask forced upon me. They connected me with something wiser within, amidst the turbulence, and I knew I would find myself again in time. But the time of waiting was one of tortured discomfort.

As I reached my teenage years that discomfort turned into a dark well of confusion, depression, and self-loathing. Being a tomboy became something to be ashamed of. The inability to understand what was happening within me became the cross of my every waking hour. I could not reconcile who I felt I was with how I was treated and perceived. My entire being, my mind, and my feelings told me I was male, yet everything on the outside, including my body, kept telling me I was female. As puberty hit, it became clear to me that my last hope, that my body would somehow correct itself, had been but a childhood dream.

A friend recently said to me, "If you had stayed in Oaxaca, you would not have survived." I realize how true that is. I feel fortunate for having been born and raised in such a beautiful land, but southern Mexico is not the most accommodating place for a young transgender guy. A few months before my 19th birthday I moved to the United States, where I found a group of people with whom I felt I belonged. I discovered I was not the only "different" person and for the first time in my life I experienced myself as "normal."

For the next two years I was in a great place with myself and with the world. I had a very positive experience at the college I attended, as I was no longer ashamed of being "different." Little by little I began coming out to my classmates and friends, and becoming more and more involved with the local LGBT community. Yet in spite of the great feeling, I still felt something was missing. I realized that I felt uncomfortable labeling myself as "lesbian," but I attributed it to internalized homophobia or some self-esteem issue that I needed to work on.

Then I met a man who would turn my world upside down. When I found out he was transgender, I became intrigued. I asked him to share his story of transformation with me. As he was telling me his life, I realized he might as well have been telling mine. This both excited and scared me. It excited me because for the first time *ever* I truly identified with someone else's experience. It scared me because I understood it meant facing something I had worked so long and hard to bury; something which would involve a major, life-changing decision. However, I knew, deep down, it was the truth about me.

It has been four years since the day I was reborn as Leon Mitchell. Some days I am just a man, other days I am a transguy or genderqueer, but I am always myself. I keep growing, changing, adapting and recreating who I am, but I am not changing due to fear, shame or a loss of self, I am coming from a different perspective: one of freedom, openness and choice. I am such a different person now from the one I used to be, it is almost as if the person I was born as never even existed. Perhaps that is why I always refer to her as "my past life." But she was real, and I still carry much of her with me; some parts I am still shedding, others I will never want to let go of.

When I look at my life as an outside observer, I marvel at the irony, absurdity, and perfection of it all. I used to resent being different and now I revel in the unique being that is me. I find great challenge and joy in the variety of experiences life has to offer. I am grateful for them all: for the culture that surrounded me as I grew up, and the one I am absorbing today; for the differing, often opposing, spiritual paths I was exposed to, and my departure and return to the One that calls me Home; and for the opportunity to experience the polarities of woman and man and their merger into my now whole being.

Age 32   Age 54

LuLu Manus is a 55-year-old transsexual woman living in Aptos, California with her wife, Kathy. LuLu is a musician, master mechanic, contractor, and aspiring writer.

Becoming LuLu—Loving God

It was a sunny Sunday morning in March 2004, a day like any other Sunday. Some people were going to church, others were going to the beach, visiting relatives, sleeping in, or doing any one of the various things one might do on such a Sunday morning. I awoke in a seriously depressed state of mind. (At that moment, I could not have predicted what a turning point the day would be.) Although I had lived fifty-two years resigned to the fact that I was a genetic male, I realized I could not keep hiding my true self.

I always dreamed about being a woman and I practiced various ways of expressing my female self. Secretly, I wore articles of women's clothing, and even ventured out wearing them from time to time, whenever I had the chance. As a child of seven, I had made little skirts for myself and hidden them under my mattress. Although I was a married man, I still secretly longed to live as a woman.

So, back to Sunday morning—a point of no return had been reached. I had started taking black-market hormones (without a prescription) and had "confessed" my female identity to my younger sister. I now faced telling my beloved wife of twenty years. I couldn't do it, no matter how many times I ran over the words in my mind. I was in a complete state of turmoil. I went to my office and wrote my thoughts down on my computer in order to make a script for what I might say. Then I began to write an honest self-assessment about how unfair I had been to myself and others; about how I had married with the thought that love could cure all.

Who I was, however, could not be "cured." Did I have the courage to change my life? I felt like someone who had been run over in the street. I put my head down on the desk and wept. I felt like a hopeless freak. Why had I been born this way? The pain was so great I just wanted to die. My thoughts turned to killing myself. My brain was so scattered, however, I could not think of how to do it. I recalled how awful I felt when my older sister was killed. How could I hurt the people I love? Trapped on all sides, I cried out to God for help.

I was not what you would call a religious person, or even a believer, but in my pain I reached out, like a drowning person, to God. I said, "Give me strength, God. Give me the words; I don't know what to say." Still weeping, I pleaded again, "Show me the way, guide me, I am lost, do with me as you will. Please help Kathy and give her strength." I hesitated, recalling that her father had just died last year, and now this.

When I felt calm, I went home to my wife and I said, "Sit down. There is something I need to tell you." Thoughts raced through Kathy's mind. What is going on? Has he found somebody else? Does he want a divorce?

I continued, "There is something I have to say that I have not told you about."

More thoughts raced wildly through Kathy's mind. Is he going to tell me he is gay? Our marriage is over?

The words finally came out, "I am a transsexual. I did a test online and it confirmed something I have felt all my life." I had shared my deepest secret. I felt a profound sense of relief.

Starting to weep, Kathy said, "So what does this mean? Do you want to leave me? Do you want a sex change operation? Where does this leave us?" I said, "I am really sorry. I have not been honest with you. This is something I have had to deal with all my life and I should have been honest from the start. I love you so much and feel so bad to hurt you like this. I don't want to leave you, but this is something I *have* to deal with. I will understand if you don't want to stay with me. This is just the way I am. I have always been a transsexual. I wouldn't choose to be this way. Why would I choose to be something which is so reviled and misunderstood? Truly, I was born this way. I should have told you but I thought love would cure me. I am really sorry I have screwed up your life as well as mine."

Kathy asked, "Does this mean you want to stay with me or do you want to be with a man?" I said, "I really want to stay with you, but only if that is what you want too."

Kathy said, "I don't know yet. We will have to find a therapist. Will you agree to go with me?"

Would I go? I loved the idea. I started thinking I would be able to get legal hormones! Hmmm, does this mean I can do surgery? How can I afford it? How will I tell my father, my in-laws, my customers, my employees, my friends? I found these thoughts embarrassing. Who would understand? Wouldn't everyone reject me? I recalled how the act of crossing gender lines was met with negativity throughout my life. My mother had made it very clear that little boys do not wear long hair and dresses. Now I was embarking on a journey to cross over and never return. I felt quite anxious.

Kathy and I interviewed three therapists by telephone and chose one. None of them had much experience working with transpeople. The one we saw told us that only one in ten couples in our situation stayed married. We wanted to save our marriage.

In therapy, we both experienced a steep learning curve. Even though I had spent years on the internet looking into the world of transpeople, I found that I held many misconceptions. I learned that transition was not only about my ability to live and present as a woman. There was also a transition required for Kathy, our friends, and our families.

I soon realized I had a responsibility to become a really good friend to Kathy, something I had largely taken for granted as a man. I had to work hard to become a good listener. I learned to find out what things were important to her and to negotiate, rather than personalize, our differences. I started to learn about the importance of good boundaries. I participated in household duties like never before.

I found that I could get hormones and medical care through my HMO—an important step in loving myself. But what would happen to our sex life? Would hormones change how I felt about Kathy? Only time would tell.

Kathy lost and had to regain her sense of self. I had been her cowboy, her dream man, her only husband. But that person was a lie. Now that person was leaving. He would be dead soon, replaced by an awkward woman trying to learn what other women had been raised to know.

In addition to redefining her sense of self, Kathy would have to work both at forgiving me for this betrayal and at accepting me in my new gender role. Could she forgive completely? She coped at first by adopting me as a kind of "teenage daughter project." I didn't know what to wear, how to sit, talk, or walk in ways that wouldn't attract stares. I didn't have a purse or shoes. All I had was a collection of cheap makeup.

It was hard, but Kathy gradually got accustomed to seeing me in women's clothing and make-up. My growing breasts were much harder for her to accept. We needed to learn new ways to love one another and to share that love in a sensitive and intimate manner. Imagine the therapist telling Kathy, "It's alright to touch LuLu's breasts."

Kathy called The Diversity Center and learned about other resources that were available to us. We both read many books to learn as much as we could about transgender issues. Through the Center, I started attending a transgender support group. In addition, we both started attending PFLAG, a support group for friends and family members of GLBT people. Through PFLAG we both became involved with Triangle Speakers, an organization comprised of people like us who help raise awareness about GLBT people. Kathy and I became willing speakers, sharing our transition experiences.

Eventually, I stopped working as a landscape contractor and found a part-time job at The Diversity Center as Trans Community Coordinator. Under a grant from the California Endowment and in partnership with Planned Parenthood Mar Monte (PPMM), we were able to bring primary health care to the local transgender community. While I worked there, the Center sponsored a conference with PPMM and Family Services Agency to help educate 125 local therapists about transgender issues. I served on the speaker panel, and Kathy and I did some role-playing to demonstrate the issues that arise for trans couples.

After eight sessions in marriage counseling, we were referred to separate therapists for individual counseling. Kathy, who in a sense had lost both men in her life, was also referred to grief counseling. Our first therapist later told me she thought that during our joint sessions, I might have been holding back in regard to discussing sex reassignment surgery (SRS). In actuality, the longer I was on hormones, the less I felt the need for SRS. Kathy and I were trying to remain in a committed relationship. I felt no need to have this invasive and expensive procedure.

As a couple, we became more involved in local GLBT events. I marched in Pride 2004 with the transgender contingent. Kathy marched with PFLAG in Pride 2005. In 2006, my trans friends and I put together a float for the Pride march featuring our rock band, "The Transistorz."

We attended an "Out In Our Faith" conference held at the Reformed Jewish temple. Local faith group leaders shared their experiences of welcoming and affirming GLBT people. I attended the Creating Change Conference in Oakland, the Transgender Leadership Summit in Southern California, and many other local events as a Diversity Center employee. I helped organize facilitator training for our transgender support groups. I continue to serve as a facilitator twice a month.

As we searched for new meanings in life, I studied meditation and became interested in finding a spiritual path. One day, I was struck by a passage in *How to Practice* by His Holiness, the Dalai Lama. He wrote that one could have a truly spiritual experience in the middle of a Mass. I was surprised. I thought about how boring church services had been in the past. That weekend Kathy and I decided to attend mass at a local Catholic church. I experienced the Mass in a completely new light, and understood the significance of the experience as never before. The Gospel readings were speaking directly to me about thoughts I had during the week. I experienced being part of a picture greater than myself. I realized God loved me just as I was, regardless of my gender.

I began to feel the Holy Spirit working in me, guiding my life in new and unexpected ways. We became church members and have been formally confirmed as Roman Catholics. The pastor has welcomed us. We have gradually come out to all of our church friends. When we are asked directly about ourselves, we share the truth. Kathy is active in several volunteer ministries and has made friends where she might have once expected to be an outcast. I am a very visible member of the music ministry, singing and playing several musical instruments at Mass every Sunday morning.

During a reading of the Gospel where Jesus asks the disciples to take up a cross and follow, I was struck with a revelation that being born a transperson was both a cross to bear and a wonderful gift. Even though our culture clings deeply to the idea of only two sexes, I have come to believe there are actually five genders: genetic male, genetic female, intersex, transman, and transwoman. As a transwoman, I feel that I have been given a unique perspective and a deep understanding.

As a practicing Christian, I am saddened to see many people misinterpreting scripture and holding to antiquated belief systems that promote transphobia and homophobia. As Roman Catholics, we have no problem reconciling religion and science. God reveals to us through scripture, science, and personal revelation.

Wouldn't it be better if we all loved one another and lived in non-judgment? If we could learn from those who are different, we would not be able to marginalize anyone. I feel that as a member of a marginalized group, I can understand all groups of people who are oppressed.

I marvel at the whole experience. Why do some people feel ill at ease in their genetic bodies? No one has a definitive answer. I recently read about an interesting experiment with frogs. Male tadpoles were subjected to estrogenic compounds, which caused them to develop into female frogs. It makes one think about how complex chemistry within the womb impacts our very being. Do extremely small chemical variations during pregnancy cause the brain to develop so that an individual's self-perception comes into conflict with their genetic gender? Can chemical variations cause similar divergences to one's sexuality as well? Perhaps someday we will have an answer.

I feel that it is preposterous to assume that God creates only males and females. We can see how complex and diversified God's work is. It is illogical that God would create diversity, and then forbid it. Scientific knowledge and God's knowledge must be one truth and can never be in conflict.

We all become victims if we continue to live in ignorance. I was a victim because I could not live as I had been genetically created. My childhood family life seemed to revolve around rigid gender roles. I could not be myself without suffering the dire consequences of shame and rejection.

When I came out as a transwoman, my father and younger sister experienced deep suffering and confusion. Today, I see them as victims as well. I know they love me dearly, but it was just very hard for them to understand who I was. Our family relationships, which had been built around gender roles, came crashing down. My younger sister, who was the first one I told, initially said that she loved me anyway. But later, she seemed very angry and distressed about it. Over time, these emotions have subsided, much to my relief.

It was a difficult time for my sister and me since our mother had recently had a massive stroke and gone into a nursing home for total care. Doctors didn't think she would live long, given the nature of the damage. She passed away after 18 months.

At her memorial, I delivered a loving eulogy, presenting for the first time as my true female self to old neighbors and family friends who were previously unaware of my transition. Jaws dropped, but everyone was loving and kind. (My sister had put out the word, it seems.)

Afterwards, my sister and father both went through a painful grieving process. There were now only the three of us from my birth family. My older sister had died, a homicide on the streets of San Francisco, back in 1994. I see now that, to my father and younger sister, it was as if I, too, had died. I believe that had I been more at ease in revealing myself as a transwoman earlier on, this type of suffering could have been minimized.

My dad has had the most difficult time adjusting to my gender change. Since he lives in another state, I came out to him on the telephone. I attempted an explanation, but he had his own ideas. He reasoned that I had been made this way by the strong women in our family. He couldn't understand that I was *born* this way, had always been this way, but had not been able to tell anyone about it. He thought I just liked to put on women's clothes. He sent me an article about local male college students who wore skirts on campus to poke fun at rigid gender roles. It hurt my feelings that my father saw my coming out as a joke or a game of dress-up. I wrote him a letter asking for respect and to please not make a joke out of me. He never replied to the letter. I realize today that he was going through various stages of grief.

At the end of the first year, however, I wanted to visit him and for him to see me in person. We drove ten hours to the town where my dad lives with his female partner. We had just pulled into the driveway, hadn't even said 'hello' or gotten into the house, when he asked, "Why do you want to be a woman?" He seemed distressed, even anguished. The visit was rocky. His partner privately explained that he had been hit very hard by my transition. My father had lost something very important to him—a son.

For many men, especially men of his generation, having a son means a great deal. Girls are okay, but sons are something special. But it's also something more, a feeling of pride in having another male in the family to relate to. I don't think he will ever completely understand the concept of having a transsexual daughter (or, should I say, son?); nor do I expect him to. He is of a time when the only transpeople anyone knew about were female impersonators. Even if I pass well, he will always see "a man in a dress."

I am lucky to have been born with a petite frame and relatively fine features. Not only that, Kathy has helped me to present well. I don't see passing as the ultimate goal, but it sure helps when I need to use the restroom. It also helps to avoid being hassled by those Neanderthals who pick on people who are different. I know my father loves me, as I love him, and that is all that is important to me in the relationship. I don't care if I pass, or not, in his mind. I will always love and respect him.

My in-laws, who live in the Midwest, have also had to make a shift. They were astonished and flabbergasted. They thought that our marriage would break up for sure. Since we only visit them once or twice a year, they have a hard time getting the pronouns, or even my name, right. I understand that it is hard to adjust when you have known someone for such a long period of time, and don't see them often.

My wife's family was very concerned about their daughter's well-being. I am sure that the love and commitment we show for each other helps put them at ease. My brother-in-law, who is an evangelical fundamentalist Christian, said he likes me even better now, because I am more fun to be around. I have had to learn not to make assumptions, even about other Christians.

I had assumed my friends would be uncomfortable with my transition, that they would no longer want my friendship. There have been many kinds of reactions, mostly positive. My good Mexican friends just laughed and said something to the effect, "You just have to be happy." The Mexican laborers I hired had the same reaction. I guess my assumptions about machismo Mexican culture were proven false.

Men's reactions varied from slightly uncomfortable, to just coming up and giving me a big kiss. Women tended to say, "Well, now you're one of us," thereby welcoming me into the world of women. Women seemed to be more accepting and most ready to share with me everything about how life is as a woman.

Although, to some, my transition seemed to be a hurried affair, as if I had come charging out of the closet, hell-bent on becoming a woman, nothing could be further from the truth. I lived most of my life stepping cautiously, carefully testing chilly waters, before I ever plunged in.

So much has changed during my lifetime—civil rights, equal rights, equal opportunity, women's rights, gay and lesbian rights, and even some advances for transpeople. Through the course of my life, I watched people struggle for equality and civil rights. And the fight goes on. A society can only be judged by how well it treats the least of us. As a transwoman, I do not enjoy the same civil rights as others. Discrimination in health care, employment, and housing still exists.

Some people hate me just because I am a transperson. My answer to them is that I am a child of God, anyone who denies me denies God himself. I know, because I denied my own self. When I accepted myself, I received the great gift of God in my life. I hope someday we all learn to love one another, no matter who or what we are.

Age 31   Age 41

Lennox Ginn is a 43-year-old transsexual man living in San Jose, California. He has had a long career in network and database engineering, and is currently a professional sales trainer. His many hobbies include: bodybuilding, marital arts, drum making, reading and muscle cars. He has mentored other transmen, transwomen and intersexed individuals since 2003.

Turned Inside Out

The earliest age I can remember not identifying with my born sex was at two years old. I recall standing in the bathroom of our home, looking at my father's shaving kit and wondering when I was going to grow my beard. I dreamed even then of having the freedom of a boy. I already knew that my sisters and their activities bored me.

I was the fourth of five children. Born in San Francisco, my older sister's birthday is a day before mine. Since she already had two little brothers, she begged my parents for a girl. My mother went into the hospital on my sister's birthday, and the next day I was born. They tell me I was normal looking and very alert.

As time went on I began to form my personality. I remember being more inclined toward my brothers' toys and things. Some of the memories are as vivid as yesterday. I can clearly recall that my patterns were masculine from the start. On my third Christmas (and birthday), my mother finally got me something I liked: a tall doll with a silver ball that the doll would throw back to you. It was the ball that I liked—I couldn't tolerate the doll past one afternoon.

I enjoyed playing hot wheels and pop guns, racing down the street and wandering too far away with my two older brothers. From a very young age I knew that my sisters were not whom I wanted to hang out with. My brothers were adventurous, always coming home with tales of the excitement they'd witnessed. They got whooped for the things they got into, but the satisfied looks on their faces told me the fun was worth the price of "the belt." I remember "manning it up" at three years old, trying to shave behind the closed bathroom door. I dabbed on my father's Old Spice and envisioned myself as a grown man.

Around the same time, I experienced my first crush. Lori was the daughter of the alcoholic couple next door. I was in love and I dreamed of marrying her. Every day I'd wait by the window hoping to catch a glimpse of her. My heart would pound when she spoke to me. I'd daydream that I'd grow up, put on a suit every day, and provide for her. I would take care of her and we'd live happily ever after.

On my 4th birthday my mother gave me my first and last pink cake. I was so upset that the cake was pink I didn't want anything to do with it. My brothers cruelly teased me about pink being a girl color. I knew then that pink wasn't my color and, once again, I felt that I was being forced to accept something I didn't like.

I was determined not to let anyone stop my growth. As I grew up, I excelled in sports and became a notorious street warrior. Then I discovered my older sister's academic books on human sexuality, and I found them extremely interesting. At eight or nine I learned about my first transsexual, Christine Jorgensen. Immediately upon seeing her transformed body, I felt relief, like there was hope. On the opposite page, there was a nameless transsexual man. He had an oversized and ill-shaped phallus. It was almost disturbing. But, it was a penis and I believed that I should have one too. I could be changed like the man in the photo. I already knew I was intended to be a boy. I was too strong, too fast and too skilled to play with the girls. This was usually my argument. Someone always got hurt playing with me. And for that I was always scolded. So, I insisted on being made a part of the activities of the other boys. If I had to, I'd force my way into the "Boys Only" clubhouses and groups my brothers and cousins formed. During this time, my mother made subtle attempts to find my "girl interests," but there was nothing girly that appealed to me. So, she allowed me to grow up uninhibited for the most part.

As puberty set in I became a tall skinny emotional disaster. I fought internally for my identity. My sexuality had already been established: I liked girls. I always have and it has always felt natural. As a child my appearance and behavior was male-like. Each year since kindergarten, a parent-teacher conference was called to inform my mother, "She is a Tomboy." They'd go on to make corrective suggestions, such as forcing me to wear dresses and other girl clothes. I'd worn boy clothes since preschool, by my own choice. I wasn't, however, allowed to cut my hair. My mother prided herself on her girls' hair. Our braids flowed down as far as our butts, so we were always the center of attention. It upset me to be called pretty and to have my hair played with. A dress in combination with the girl hair might fix the problem, may have been their thinking. Year after year these conferences occurred. Each time my mother explained that I was a hyperactive child and it was best to just let me wear the pants.

I was determined to develop for myself and not for anyone else. I boxed and played baseball, soccer, football and karate as the only girl on the team or in the club. I was actually a nice well-rounded child. Then, in the 6th grade, I was devastated by the physical changes of puberty. My mother insisted that I wear a bra; I refused until they were so big that they were obvious titties. My father was sent in to talk to me about the bra. He explained that bras protected and supported the breasts. Eventually I just gave in. At that point I did everything I could to flatten them out. I kept them covered to the top of my pecs and left my shirts unbuttoned to highlight muscles like the men I saw on television.

Before the breasts came, I'd worked my way up and down the street "playing house" with every girl on the block and around the corner. I'd pull my ponytail tight and, shirtless, I'd ride a little bit further each time to find new girls who didn't know me as a female. I'd tell them my name was Allen and that my mom liked my hair long because we were Indian and Black. They fell for my story and we'd do our thing, sometimes right there on the sidewalk. Then, like a boy, I'd ride off and never see them again. So I guess you could say I started cross-dressing as a male around age seven, in order to socialize affectionately with the girls.

When puberty came, the titties broke me. They took my confidence away and made me ashamed of myself. I became angry and rebellious. I went through what I call a "Dark Mood" and I felt hopeless. No matter how much I tried to will it away the femaleness was taking me over. When I realized I couldn't stop it, I wanted to die. By then, I could barely take being referred to as a girl. My mother was mostly supportive, but when it came to church, I was required to wear a dress. I felt deeply ashamed of being seen in a dress and each time I had to wear one, I was depressed for months.

On my 12th birthday, when my mother asked me what I wanted for a gift, I asked her for a sex change. She said, "Girl… No!" I remember the look in her eye—she knew we would come back to this someday. Believing my fate was sealed though, I went through that year resigned to living the rest of my life in the wrong body. The way I saw it was that I had a male brain that didn't match my female body. It was a living hell.

Sometime the next summer, I was forced to wear a dress to my Grandfather's appreciation ceremony. He was a respected clergyman. It was a great honor to him and to the family for him to be recognized. The night before, I was terrified by the thought of putting on another dress. It was so painful, so humiliating and so wrong for me. I cried real tears as I tried to reason with my mother that my brothers didn't have to wear dresses, so why did I? She insisted that it was because I was a girl. I didn't call myself a boy, but I certainly was not a girl! That night, faced with the shame of the next day and being made to appear in front of hundreds of people in a dress, and having been told yet once more that I was a girl, I took an entire bottle of Valium. Perhaps it was because the expiration date had passed by a couple of years, I awoke the next morning. I had a stomachache and a pounding head, but I still had to put on that fucking dress. I knew then that I had to let my hopes go.

If I couldn't kill myself to be free, I would live out the rest of my days as a lesbian female and give up my quest for a sex change. I went through my high school years playing sports and honing my lesbian identity. I had girlfriends and a few boyfriends. I was outed during my 9th grade year and ran with it, choosing to come all the way out. The other gay students decided that I'd be their leader and we formed the first unofficial gay student club at our suburban school. I had a girlfriend and we created disturbances by acting like the straight couples: holding hands, kissing and sharing other intimacies on campus. I had a ball.

When summer came I was stuck at home, only to be ridiculed by my siblings. Ever since I was nine years old, my older sister would hold kid-only "Family Meetings" during the summers and school holidays. These meetings were to determine if I was a "man." Even my little sister was given a vote. I was barred from the meetings until after my older sister's summation. Through the closed door, I'd hear each kid be called upon to make his or her case. Their "evidence" deemed me to be male. My older sister had given me many names over the years: Jim, Bob, Dave, Steve, Manly and, my all-time favorite, "Man." I would cry and defend myself with fighting passion, insisting that I was just a tomboy. I pressed on throughout the years and with each family meeting I became stronger. I eventually learned to stop becoming involved in them. I made myself unavailable for their mean bullshit.

I continued developing as a girl and continued to make failed attempts to act like a woman. I spent 11 years in a relationship with a woman who told me she thought I was transgendered, but I refused to discuss it with her. I was terrified of the way transgendered people were treated back then. And I had vowed never to make the physical corrections I needed while my mother was still alive. I could never hurt her that way, I believed then.

When my ex-partner moved away with our daughter, I experienced a major life change. For many years I had tried to live as a soft butch for my lover. As I became more independent, that didn't fit for me anymore. I began dressing and trying to pass as a long-haired soft male at night. I looked like a tall skinny boy, just like when I was a kid. I became a little bit comfortable again. Then I progressed into a short-haired stud, pumping iron and wearing very baggy pants. I could pass as male by my upper chest muscles alone. For many years I worked out beside people who believed I was male and didn't realize I was female-bodied until I transitioned.

As a lesbian, I had always had a difficult time understanding much of what women truly thought. It had always been difficult to get my girlfriends to understand that I really couldn't relate to some of the things they were going through. They'd always tell me, "You should know better, because you are a woman." I'm the only one who knew the truth. And I could barely admit it for most of my life—not since I was 12, when my hopes were crushed, having been told I couldn't have a sex change for my birthday present. I think I just started waiting for death to resolve the issue. I had begged my mother to promise she'd never bury me in women's clothes. I told her, "It would be like going to hell." As supportive as she'd been in giving me my choice of toys and clothes, she remained in denial of my rejections of femaleness and declarations of my maleness. As I became more masculine she'd refer to me more frequently as "girl." I shrieked and protested every time. It was a direct insult. I wanted the status and acknowledgment of a boy—the freedom of being myself.

In 2003 I made a decision to overhaul my life. I asked my girlfriend to move out. She had been the most emasculating person I'd ever had in my life. I asked her to leave to free myself. I wanted control over my life and my feelings. Nor could I go on with committing to "not while my mother is still alive." My mother had survived two brain aneurysm surgeries. God clearly walks with her. Every day of her life, since the second surgery, she wakes to embrace her life, her kids and her God. If my mother's condition could be repaired, why couldn't mine?

For bodybuilding I had begun a cycle of steroids and loved the physical, mental and positive self-esteeming effects it had on me. For the first time in my life, I felt some sense of balance. For years I had trained as hard as, often harder than, many of the men at my gym. I would increase my strength right along with them, always seeming to pump one plate more than the guy next to me. But, the guy next to me was almost always bigger. So during this renewal time in my life, I decided to begin steroids. Immediately I felt its effects. The rush of life pumped through my veins, my body, my mind and my loins. I was on fire it seemed. I worked at a car dealership. My sales were my highest average ever and I grossed about $15,000 that month. In the gym, I broke plateau after plateau as I pumped past men who had been much bigger than me for years. My muscles exploded and I was the shit. My theory had been correct: I was the same as the guys, I just needed the same hormone balance they had. Chemically, I was now equal. At home, I became more organized. I began to save money and spend wisely. I was returning to life. The changes would make me the happiest I'd been in years.

With this great happiness came some side effects. I was aggressive. I fought a muscle-bound man over an insult on the car lot. And whooped his ass. (We are still friends.) I also developed yeast infections and the amount of discharge caused me a lot of concern. I was using the steroids for approximately three months when I entered my doctor's office for gyno-related issues. I approached the registration desk, handed the receptionist my medical card and stood there tapping my fingers as staff members slowly poured from the back to the hallway behind the reception area. They came out to tell me that I must have been looking for the Urology Department across the way. And they were saying it over and over. I was embarrassed. I brought out my driver's license, my car sales license and anything else with my name on it. I slammed them on the desk to prove that it was I, that I was a woman and that I had an appointment in that department on that day and at that time with Dr. X! I even pulled out my "Black Woman" head swirl, eye roll and index-finger-in-the-face action. I pounded my fist and screamed at them. When I finally got back to see my new doctor, I informed her that I was on steroids. She looked like she was thinking, "No Shit!" She asked if I was transgender and I told her no. I was still afraid to admit it. My blood panel said that my testosterone level was 1600. According to Hudson's FTM Resource Guide, normal test levels of combined bound and free testosterone in male bodies can range anywhere from 300-1100 ng/dl (nanograms per deciliter). Plus, my cholesterol was too high. It would take three more months, but I decided to stop using the steroids. I then switched to over-the-counter Andros until they were outlawed as class 3 steroids. (They were Testosterona Para Los Perros, which in English translates to Veterinarian Testosterone for Dogs!) Even though there were bad side effects like extremely rapid hair growth, even faster hair loss, almost unbearably torturous sex drive, anger and rage to say the least, there were also positives. The greatest benefit I observed was that testosterone made me feel more balanced. I could see that if I were injecting regular doses, I would evolve through the physical and overall changes in me.

So, about a year after starting two forms of testosterone enhancement drugs, I asked my gyno to put me on testosterone. She asked the questions: What gender did I identify as? Did I feel I was born in the "wrong body"? (I prefer "born with a male brain in a female body.") She set a therapy appointment for me and I started "corrective testosterone treatment therapy" about a month later. So I began my first official female-to-male hormone injections.

When I made this decision to transition from a female into a male, I evaluated my entire life. I thought of everything. Should I move? Should I tell my employer, my family, the gym and every other place I frequented? Would I need to relocate and create an entirely new life somewhere else?

Despite living in a big city, when I searched for someone to talk with about my gender issues, there was no one available who was willing to be a resource. I have always been bold and aggressive, so I decided to stay where I lived and educate others by transitioning in the open.

I changed my usage name at work. I was the number one salesman at the number one Subaru dealership in the U.S. They accommodated anything I needed and would always offer more. It was a male-dominated dealership and I was the only female. Previously I had worked for one month at a Chevrolet dealership, where I was not as successful. However, I learned from the successful salesmen at Chevy how to make my money at Subaru. I learned to relax and be myself. Although I was charming and very persuasive, the customers were extremely confused about my gender. I wasn't a genderqueer, but I was working only as an implied male. So changing my name at work was a major benefit. Without the distraction of the female name, the customers were more easily pushed into the sale. I observed and mimicked the other salesmen. The boss liked me and made certain I was treated with respect. He wouldn't tolerate comments regarding my gender or sexuality, but everything else was fair game. If the guys were fighting over customers or defending the dealership against an unruly customer, I was right in there with the rest of the men. I was treated no differently than any other man working there. I learned a lot about being a man both from my co-workers and my customers. And for that I gave my all.

Then, I was recruited away by an exotic, luxury and sports car dealership. And I left for the promise of $20,000 averages, luxury demos and a direct promotion to Internet Manager. I had not yet begun testosterone therapy. I was there two days when I realized they had lied. Now I was trapped because I needed to stay and wait for my insurance to kick in. After months of having my deals snatched from me, having to demand my back pay, pleading with the sales manager to fix the furnace in the building where I was relocated and being referred to as bitch on a couple of occasions, they "laid me off." They claimed they had sold the building. The sales manager told me of the layoff five minutes after I spoke "privately" with the outside benefits representative. My sales manager overheard my conversation with the benefits rep. He heard me telling the benefits rep. that I was transgendered. He heard the questions regarding my coverage and the admission that I would soon be having a hysterectomy. He overheard these things because I was forced to have my interview on the sales floor. I left with the reason for layoff written at my request. Of course they had lied.

I found another job immediately and settled in quickly. I was at my new job for about one month when friends and family began calling me one after the other asking if I was okay. It turns out, the dealership that had laid me off was blown up and it was all over the news. PG&E had hit a pipe leading to the gas furnace I had complained about for months, the one they refused to fix. The building had burned to the ground and people were injured. I had previously filed a lawsuit for discrimination. The case was quickly settled, as any defense they had prepared was dismantled by the news footage of the owner's declaration that it was his dealership and building. Things felt rectified for a change. And my life continued to blossom.

I was so happy to finally be labeled properly, "Transgender." I was excited to have some hope of feeling like a regular man. I didn't wait for the hormones to do their job. I got right to work and came out swinging. I began with the gym. What better place to transition right in the open? It had the perfect conditions—people there were familiar with me. These people had seen me for at least a year as a butch woman. I was a hard-hitting female. I'd walk through the doors of an establishment and the room would freeze. At the gym, I worked out for three years in shorts, a sports bra and a tank top. I would never bind at the gym as I needed to breathe deeply while working out and was afraid I'd pass out if I were binding. Not long after the testosterone was introduced, I blew up like some of the bigger boys at the gym. Once my facial hair grew the new gym members no longer noticed the flattened-out breasts beneath my pecks. I kept my body competition-ready for three years with the intent to have a beautiful male chest. Every year, six and sometimes seven days a week, I trained. I trained heavy nine months a year and moderate to heavy the three months of summer. In 2005 I had my hysterectomy. It was a difficult but exciting time. It was as if the thing that made me female was finally removed. My life has changed drastically since the absence of estrogen. When my chest was reconstructed in 2006 and the bandages removed, I knew my dream had come true. The pain of the surgery was nothing compared to the pain of the stares and the giggles I endured through the in-between years of transition. I finally felt complete. I have since legally changed my name and gender status with the state and federal governments. I am not certain if I'll have further surgeries, but am evaluating the Centurion Release. This is a procedure that incorporates the man's natural clitoris with other natural body fillers to provide girth, and a tendon release to provide natural length. This procedure may be the best choice for me as I am a well-endowed transman.

Age 3   Age 28

Renee Byers is a 28-year-old woman living in Santa Cruz, CA.

Finding Her Way

All of life is a transition from one state to the next: away from what repulses us and toward what attracts us.

Early on I knew that I was different and the gender I was born with was not for me. There are several pictures of me taken at age two or three wearing a diaper and my mother's bra. A few years later there's another photo of me in a makeshift dress with a little purse at my side; still another photo at my grandparents' house, in my grandmother's shoes and purse with a scarf around my head.

My first memories formed around the time my sister was born. Together we grew up surrounded by cornfields and woods in rural Ohio. Our parents' large yard and the woods behind our house was the playground for our games. Lacking other children in the neighborhood to play with, my sister and I were best of friends. With her I was able to play the roles that came naturally to me, for example, in dress-up games we'd both be princesses, completely oblivious to the gender stigma attached to my gown. I knew that I was a boy, but, because I'd not yet had a lot of contact with boys, I didn't understand exactly what that meant.

It wasn't until I reached school-age that I lost my childhood innocence. The boys didn't like that I didn't act like they did. I wasn't particularly boyish and I played with the girls. In kindergarten I encountered the strange routine of putting children into two lines, a boys' line and a girls' line, in order to go to the library or to recess. The boys in my class were quite adamant that I should be in the girls' line... and that was fine with me but the teacher insisted I should be in the boys' line. I started to feel I had been thrust into a strange world. The other children spoke their minds, without the delicate tact that adults might use, and their opinions grew more cruel and vocal as we progressed through school.

By the second grade the other children learned some words that I had not, such as "Fag," "Homo," and "Gay." They would roar with laughter when they asked me what those words meant and I could only answer with a shrug. "You like boys!" they would tease. Was that what was wrong with me? No, it was something deeper, beyond the dualism of sexual orientation and attraction, it was something inborn. I played the female roles in my fantasy world. I envied my sisters' movement through life; they got the toys I wanted and got to do the things I wanted to do. It was easy to pretend when I was younger, before the wedge of puberty drove the sexes apart.

During my childhood we attended Methodist church. There I was introduced to God, and it was to Him each Sunday, and most nights before I fell asleep, that I would pray, "Make me a girl, or let me die." Despite my prayers, I continued to wake up, very much alive and very much a boy. Over time, the division between what I was and what I wanted to be widened, and a seed of resentment began to grow in me. I hated myself for being what I was. I hated my peers and their judgments of me. The anger spilled over into my family life and our relationships suffered. Silently I accepted the other children's judgment that I was gay, never fully understanding what it meant. The impossible desire to be female became overshadowed with the reluctant acceptance that I was gay.

At 12, my emotional endurance was exhausted. The verbal and physical abuse from other kids had continued day after day, until one day in 7th grade when the teacher left the room to speak with someone in the hall. Without warning, the boy in front of me turned around and punched me in the face, something that had never happened before. Despite the pain and shock I calmly got up, went into the hall to find the teacher, and explained what just transpired. That night, I hid in my room vowing to never go to school again. I confessed to my parents that I was being teased at school but did not tell them why. How could I? I was ashamed of the secret misnomer that I was gay, as well as the secret of my impossible aspirations to be a girl.

Arrangements were made for me to be transferred to a small private Christian school in town. At first the love and acceptance I found there was overwhelming. Immediately I began to follow and believe the things they followed and believed, not only because they were required of me to attend the school, but also to be accepted by all the new people in my life. However, while the external abuse had subsided, a new kind of abuse stepped up in its place. I quickly learned at the school's religious services that God did not like homosexuals. No wonder He had ignored my prayers! My young heart was now torn between the desires to do right by God and the unavoidable desires that were very similar to being gay!

Puberty struck me late, but, oh did it strike! I became very sexually repressed, denying any and all "sinful" thoughts that I had. Nevertheless they did not stop, and I became resigned to my fate that I would burn in hell. Every time I thought "sinful" thoughts about a boy, I felt as if I had crucified the savior I so loved. Caught in a cycle of self-hatred, my anger and resentment only grew.

After graduation the religious fervor which had grabbed my naive heart began to subside. Without the weekly sermons of hellfire, the fear of disappointing God faded to a dull roar. I still thought there was something wrong with me, but now it was society who was telling me that, and it was society I felt I was disappointing. In college I met lots of different people, some of whom identified as gay, yet the years of self-hatred and shame kept me silent even in their presence.

I bought myself some books on homosexuality. They were written from the perspective that one could change his or her sexual "preference." I thought they would contain the cure to wash away my shame. Up until this point I'd guarded the secret of my sexuality with my life, feeling that if anyone knew this was how I truly felt, my life as I knew it would be over. Shortly after, my mother found the book and my life did change.

My parents confronted me one evening and, terrified, I confessed that I was "confused." Still I hid my darkest secret. Out of love, my parents took me to a therapist who, luckily, was supportive of homosexuality and suggested that I attend some services at a "gay church" in town. In my first therapy session I remember her asking me if I'd ever wanted to be a woman. Out of fear, and the belief that changing my gender was impossible, I lied to her and said no. In hindsight I wonder how my life would've been different if I had said yes.

That Sunday I started to attend the United Church of Christ. There I met openly gay and lesbian Christians who welcomed me with open arms and hearts. Until this point God and homosexuality had been diametrically opposed, yet there I made peace with the concept of God. I found a God who was much bigger than the one I had known in school. However, a few months later, God and I parted ways (though She has since returned in Her many glorious forms!)

For the first time in life I found myself free. Free from my long guarded secrets. However, the newfound exploration into my sexuality left me unsatisfied. It was other gay men that I supposed I wanted, yet I was just as unhappy with them as they were with me! "You are too feminine!" they would tell me. However, this brief foray into homosexuality taught me that there were other ways of being. I saw drag shows. I met transgendered people. I realized that a sex change was possible, not by God's help, but by one's own strength and determination.

Turning to the internet for research I decided that it was possible, even for me, to make a gender transition. I had no idea of the blood and pain and tears that would be required, but neither was I aware of the joys that awaited me on the other side. Once again I "came out" to my parents. I finally had a word to express who I thought I was—transgendered. None of us could fully grasp what I was undertaking, but my parents, and even my grandfather, offered to support me. I found another therapist, and answered her honestly when she asked her questions. She provided me with a referral to begin hormones, and I began the dreadful process of electrolysis. I started to wear feminine clothing, even though the end result was most depressing: no surgery could take away my height of 6'3".

Through research I discovered a doctor in San Francisco who was reshaping the skulls of male-to-female transsexuals through a process called Facial Feminization Surgery (FFS). Instantly I knew this was what I needed to counteract the very masculine bone structure with which puberty had left me. This decision seemed the hardest on my mother, who was frightened by the fact that the surgery would be irreversible. I think she also feared that the results would make me look radically different and that people would notice. Of course, this was exactly why I was doing it, but, to her, it would mean that I could no longer show my face in our small town.

In the months leading up to FFS, I, too, wondered if I would recognize myself after it was done. I made the decision to move to California before my FFS, because I knew that I could never thrive in Ohio. Before the surgery, I didn't pass, therefore I rarely dressed as a female. After the surgery, and its dramatic results, I began to pass almost immediately. A new state, a new name, a new face, and a new life lay before me.

My words fail me now when I try to explain this feeling to people who haven't experienced it themselves. It's the feeling of peace you experience when the thing that you've longed for as long as you've had desire finally comes to pass. The intense self-loathing of my past has been replaced by self-love! I feel whole now, even though there is always transition ahead.

Yes, all of life is a transition from one state to the next, but dread has been replaced by wonder. Frenzied prayers to God for an immaculate sex-change or death have been replaced by thankful adoration to a Goddess of Possibility.

Age 26   Age 38

Stu Doogan loves to rock out in a tranny band, goes camping as much as possible and has lots of crafty-arty projects going on at all times. He lives in "Tranny Cruz" Santa Cruz, California.

Interview with Stu

Q: Start out by telling us a little about your family.

A: I grew up with my mom, dad and older brother in New England; Massachusetts and Connecticut. My father was a congregational minister and my mother was a school teacher. I grew up in the church, so to speak, because that was Dad's gig and that is how we lived. I lived in a parsonage and I was the preacher's kid. I went to prep school in Connecticut from 7th to 12th grade. It was a very small, intimate and intense school. We all got along well in my family. My brother was very quiet and mellow. I think I bugged him, being a little sister and wanting to do the things he did. But overall, he was pretty patient with me. We never really fought except for

101

maybe a handful of times. I think that was really cool, having an older sibling that did not pound on me.

Q: When and how did you first notice issues with your gender?

A: Immediately. My earliest memories. I remember having to wear girls' clothes and having fits about it. I especially hated church, because (and I know this is totally cliché) I had to wear a dress and it was a really big deal. I would dread it and then have tantrums when I had to go. I was such a good kid most of the time, except when they were trying to shove me into a dress. (My mother and I were just talking about it this summer, like what a scene it was and how I was such a cranky kid at church.) I didn't like church anyway, but mostly I was just really uncomfortable in a dress.

My favorite Halloween was when I was five or six. I was a hobo and I got to wear a suit jacket and tie. I was so proud and felt really distinguished! Other times I would sneak my brother's clothes, Boy Scout or Cub Scout uniform, anything that was a boy identity.

I honestly felt like I was a boy ever since I was little little little. I don't remember a time when I didn't think it.

Q: How did people react? How did your parents deal with it?

A: I think I'm lucky because my parents were very open-minded and they have become even more open-minded. They weren't hippies, but they were teachers of the hippies. There are also queer people in my family, who are out, and, not that queer equals tranny, but in my case, it went hand in hand. Because of the youth groups they ran and the hippies they taught, my parents hung out with a real hodgepodge of people.

At first, they did not understand the dress thing. Then they saw that I was a tomboy and they started letting me wear my hair short and buying me toys that were more boy toys like GI Joe. I didn't want the Barbies. I wasn't really allowed to have guns but I could play Lone Ranger and Tonto because my dad loved Lone Ranger and Tonto too. So I was allowed to play Cowboys and Indians, as long as there weren't guns.

In high school I think they were a little relieved because I wasn't boy crazy, and, unlike most of the students my mother taught in her high school, I had a good sense of who I was. I think my parents totally rock because they were great people. And they understand me even more now that I am out and transitioned. They look back and say, "Oh, in that time you were doing such and such because that is how you were expressing your male self. We didn't understand it then and we thought you were just being a tomboy or a lesbian or whatever, so we just allowed you to do what we thought was within appropriate limits."

So, for the most part they let me act and look like a tomboy. For formal occasions, however, I still had to dress feminine to some degree. I could wear a feminine suit, which was an okay enough compromise at the time, though I didn't really like it.

Q: How did the gender issues play out in your adolescence, with peers and teachers?

A: The school I went to was so small, everybody got to know everybody really well. It was like a prep school for kids who got kicked out of other prep schools because they were naughty or whatever. There were a lot of kids from New York City and from all over the world. Consequently, there were a lot of queer kids in my school. When I got there, they already had an "out and loud" crowd so I just kind of fell into that queer culture right in 7th grade. They were accepting and I was kind of a jock tomboy, and the girl sports in the school were doing really well because there were so many dykes.

I wasn't necessarily "out" because I hadn't been hiding my sexuality, just my gender. I just felt very boyish. So here was a group of girls that liked girls, and I was allowed to be who I was in that group. I thought, okay, well, maybe I am just a dyke and that's okay. I still felt kind of uncomfortable in my body, but I was expressing myself in a masculine way and being accepted. So, I had a pretty decent high school experience.

I did have one rough moment. It was after my prom. I had worn a tuxedo and had two dates: a boy and a girl, and we were just friends. (By the time I became a junior, the school had gotten more conservative. The preppy handbook was out and it had become really critical to be more "in the box." A lot of the freaky queer kids had moved on, graduated or been kicked out. I was just about the last of this group of people.) So I wore this tuxedo to the prom and the next day at school, the Chaplain gave me crap about it, saying I was ruining the image of the school. Basically, I got a warning to keep my shit together. That was really the only threat I got. But at that point, I had been there for four years and they weren't going to kick me out.

Q: What about later in young adulthood, what transpired with your gender then?

A: In high school I saw a television special on transsexuals. I had always known that you could change from male-to-female but had no idea that there were female-to-male trannys out there. I didn't think it was possible. Then I saw this show and I thought, "Oh my god, that's ME! I am a freak, but oh my god, that is cool!" But then I kind of shoved the whole idea aside, though I never ever forgot about it. I don't know if the documentary was well done or not, but it helped me just knowing that FTMs were out there.

So when I was a young adult, I lived as a big ol' butch dyke. I was really out, loud, and proud. However, I kept looking out the corner of my eyes for the trannys, thinking, "Where are you?" I got really involved in the queer community and there were plenty of tranny ladies but no tranny boys. I was identifying as butch, kind of a very masculine woman. But I knew I was really a boy. And I dated femmy lesbian ladies. And then dildos became the thing. We discovered it was okay for a dyke to have a dick. And I think that completely changed the queer community. And not only queers but everyone else because it was positive to use dildos and not necessarily just a hetero thing to have sex in that way.

Q: So when did you decide to change gender? How did that come about?

A: It came about when I was working at a women's bookstore. I was talking with a friend of mine. She felt very similar to the way I did and we kind of came out to each other: "Hey, I feel like a boy," "Me, too, and I don't know what to do about it."

It had to be maybe less than six months later when *Stone Butch Blues*, by Leslie Feinberg, came out. We were working in the bookstore, so we all read it right away and then Leslie Feinberg came to our store and spoke. This was when we all got our first dosage of, oh my god, here is a real tranny. And soon several people started coming out and talking about it. I think I was 26, and I was really really nervous. There was a group of us that formed a meeting so we could talk about tranny things. That is where I first met some of my close tranny friends. It was great just to talk about stuff, like how do we get hormones? How do we support one another? What the hell are we doing? This was the first time in my life that I felt comfortable enough talking about it without feeling, you know, weird. And without worrying about people thinking, "You are just a butch dyke. You don't really want to be a man." Because by then it was, yes, I want to be a man.

And then soon after meeting Leslie Feinberg we met Loren Cameron. That's right when Loren's book *Body Alchemy* came out. And that is where it all kind of gelled because here was a person who had actually transitioned. Leslie Feinberg had been more about questioning gender, as in: are you identifying as male or female *today*? For him/her (depending on the day) it was like, for this period of time I was male, for this period of time I was female. Whereas Loren Cameron was "I'm a dude now, a *dude* dude." Wow! He showed us his chest and his surgery and talked all about it. He didn't hold anything back. We drilled him with questions.

Q: How about the concrete decisions to get on hormones and do surgery? What was it like telling people what you were going to do?

A: It took me a long time to make the decision to get on hormones. I wanted to so bad, but I was really scared. Medically, I did not really understand it. Plus, I was a singer and I was really worried that my voice would change, which it would, and I wouldn't be able to sing. I had my identity as this kind of butch dyke-y folk singer that I was really comfortable with, but I wanted to personally move on and be something else. It really took a lot of just sitting with it—and watching my friends' transition. I was feeling more and more uncomfortable in my female body and I was seeing how comfortable they were becoming in their changing bodies. It was like everywhere I turned I got the green light, so to speak. My partner at the time was amazingly supportive. She was like, "Yeah I can see it, it's there when you are ready for it, and everybody will be okay with it when you are." So I decided I was going to take hormones, but I needed to tell my parents before I did it. I also decided I was going to have chest surgery. All my friends were like "Yeah, yeah, it's great, no worries, we got you." But I was still worried about my parents.

On my 30th birthday, I talked to them. I had previously sent them a letter, which they had received, and they said, "You know what, we are not surprised at all and we're really glad that you are being honest with yourself, and moving forward. Let us know how we can be helpful—it will be a transition for us too, so be patient—we will do whatever we can." They have been amazing.

I was working with my friend, piano tuning, so it wasn't a big deal at work. It was just the two of us. But I wasn't making much money so I had to get a normal job. I went into my new job as a female, but I had already changed my name to Stu. They just thought I was a girl named Stu. Then I came out to them and told them what I was going to do. They were like "That's great, that's awesome, cool." They thought they were hiring a lady but ended up with another dude. And they were okay with it, actually they were great.

My insurance lady was matter-of-fact. "Okay, let's change things on your paperwork." It has been golden. I am incredibly lucky and grateful for my family and friends and my partner. I didn't have to fight. I only had to fight with myself, just leaving the comfort zone of living one way your whole life and now deciding to live a different way.

Q: What was it like for you when you were in the "in-betweener" stage?

A: I just couldn't stop thinking about everything; I was obsessed with looking in the mirror. I was constantly bugging my friends who had already begun their transitions, asking them questions. What's it like? What do you do now? They were all in a euphoric state, amazed at their sex drive and their energy. But I just couldn't get over the hump to actually do it, even though I really wanted to. I wanted to see what really happened to them, not just know about it from a book. Once I started seeing this one and that one becoming happy with their changes, I thought, "You know what? I am coming… here I come. Thanks for pulling me along guys." They were really like, come on, it's cool, jump in the water, it's safe. But I was a little scared just cuz it was so different and so permanent.

Q: What were you afraid of?

A: That's a good question. Because everything was going smoothly, you know, it wasn't like I was going to lose my job or my home or my relationship. I wasn't going to lose my family or my friends. It was just me being a Scorpio and thinking about things until I could get to the point where I could jump in. I was afraid of losing my voice, musically, and it's not like I had a really great voice, but it was my voice. And when I finally started taking hormones, I completely lost my singing voice. For a long time I couldn't sing. I still can't sing the range I used to be in, which is really weird. I have a totally different range now which I have become comfortable in and actually like better. I was nervous about that and I was also nervous because I was a kind of public figure in the queer community, working in a café and being a known musician. I was the little queer rock star and everybody had their opinion, and everybody commented. I was under the public eye, so to speak. That was a little nerve racking so I definitely went into hiding a bit. Most people in the community were cool, though. There were a few who thought it sucked, like, "Where are all you dykes going?" And then they got over it. Most of the people have since apologized. A couple of people haven't. But I think I was just scared of change in general.

Q: Any funny memories you have from the different stages you went through in changing gender?

A: Everything's funny. The first time your voice cracks, the first time you sprout hair on your back. It's all the weird little firsts. For one, I looked really young. "Oh, sonny!" I have tons of those but the first few were a riot. I would totally play into it. I got to be an actor in two roles and that was a lot of fun, just fooling around and screwing with people. Every now and then, gently putting someone in their place, "Oh, you know, I am not a girl," or "I am not a boy," or "I'm both!" I still have that kind of Queer-Nation-style of political in-your-faceness. Early on, visually I was presenting as both. I was an effeminate gentleman or a masculine lady. I have really young looking cherub cutesy pinky cheeks, a squeaky clean apple pie look, which is annoying. I don't think I'd had chest surgery yet, but I think I was on hormones and my voice had changed and I had facial stubble. So I could play tricks. There was one time, at work, and I haven't done it since, but there was this one dude and I was talking with his wife about something and he says, "Well, you know how women are." He was just being a dick, just being really rude to his wife, and being all chummy and boys-clubby with me and I just wasn't into it and was totally on her side. So I just decided they had to have their minds blown, and I say, "Yeah, actually I am one." I lost that sale and have never seen them since. In that moment, I just thought, "screw it." And that was fun. Maybe not too professional, but he deserved it.

Q: How has life been different for you living perceived as female versus living perceived as male?

A: I was just talking about this with my friends, yesterday, when we were riding our bikes around. One friend was saying how she feels gender vibes are thrown around her or at her. She looks kind of goofy, like a cartoon, with her pink hair, but it's just her style and persona. When I was a dyke, I had a flat top and combat boots and I was totally punk-y looking, not really punk but a completely out dyke. It was so obvious. And I would get vibes and looks all the time. I've always dealt with that though, because I was so boyish growing up and never the girl I was "supposed to" look like. Then, in the last five years, I haven't had that attention and I have been able to fly under the radar, so now I feel sort of sneaky about everything, like I am a spy. I have seen both sides and I know how they both work. But I no longer get people looking at me, because I look normal to them, a normal guy. They would never know that I was not always the guy they think I am.

Q: Does that feel like a relief or a loss?

A: A little of both. Right now for me it's more of a relief because I get to just flow in this body without having everybody look at me. When I am performing, however, I like to, you know, dork out. There is my stage persona and there is the rest of me. Offstage, I like to garden, go hiking, and paddle in my kayak and blend in. So it's kind of a relief. Maybe I'm just getting older. I am not the center of attention anymore and that's fine. It's so much easier for me to get through the world now. Simple things like going to the store and buying groceries—I don't have to look people in the eye to make them stop staring at me. I can just buy groceries. That's different. It's easier. I like it. I am definitely way more comfortable in this body. Absolutely. Way more than in the other.

Q: How did you feel when you had the chest surgery? Did you have any ambivalence about it?

A: By the time I decided, I was just very clear. I got it done and felt better instantly. It was just a matter of getting the money together. If I had known when I was 20 all of what I knew when I was 26, I would have done it then or even younger. Having a role model when I was younger would have been great but I accept my path was what it was. Chest surgery was amazing for me. It hurt, it was expensive, but so what. It was worth it.

Q: Is there anything you learned about being in the male world that surprised you; anything that you didn't expect?

A: Men are pigs, disgusting baboons. I learned how truly little they respect women and that was shocking. I learned how they can be just as petty as junior high school girls talking behind each other's backs. They are so competitive. And rude. Men see men as threatening. And they have their little swagger and their little bubble in which they pretend that they are oh so mighty. This is not all of them, of course, but there are a lot like that. Much of it is posturing for women's attention but a lot of it is just to "out bro the bros." It's so stupid. I don't see it so much in older men but I do in younger men and men my age. I think the next generation is better. I feel that one of my secret roles as a dude is to tell dudes not to "dis" the ladies and to have more love and compassion.

Q: How do men respond?

A: I think my personality is very non-threatening and I feel like a lot of guys are comfortable talking with me about their feelings because of that. If someone is just talking smack, I say, "You know that's not nice" or "Why you gotta do that? That guy is cool (or that lady is great)." I just kind of spin their criticisms back around and say, "I like gay people" or "I like that guy's clothing 'cuz I think he looks cute in it" or whatever. I think the guys I work with are way happier now that they have a more positive perspective. They hang around me and they like it and it has lightened them up a lot. But customers, if I have customers that are being too sexist, I totally call them on it in a non-threatening dude way. If I were a dyke they would be completely threatened by what I was saying. But when a guy tells the guys, "Hey that's not cool, come on, are you living in the 50s?" they stop and think. I'm not blaming and being a jerk about it, I'm coming from a place of compassion and kindness. I don't hate you for what you said, but what you said was stupid. It's bull and this is why.

Q: So where are you now with your gender and your body?

A: I have to tell you this funny thing. This morning, I trimmed the hair on my back to try to convince it to grow out of my face, somehow. These are my challenges! I have more hair on my back than anywhere else. But mainly, I am really happy and comfortable, super comfortable. I need to get in shape, but that's just laziness, nothing like, "Oh my god, I can't stand it." I want a little bit more plastic surgery, a revision on my chest surgery. It's still the best decision I ever made in my life.

Q: How do you think your life would have been different if you had not transitioned?

A: I can't imagine it. That's the thing. I think I would have never stopped "what if-ing" myself. I probably would have driven myself nuts with it. I can't imagine being 38 years old as a woman (I've been living as male for eight years and on hormones for longer). It wasn't like I was unhappy before… that was the thing, I was really a happy person, but I think I would probably be depressed now because I'd still be uncomfortable in my body. You know it's just simple things like walking around, it's just more comfortable now, and it's hard to explain. It's the really tiny things that make a big difference in my life. I don't know how much longer I could have stood it. But I'll never have to find that out.

Q: So is there anything that you would like the people of the world to know about trannys or about gender?

A: There is no definite line between male and female. It seems like more and more people are expressing, at least in pop culture, their effeminate side or their masculine side, no matter what type of body they have. I would rather have those lines be blurry. I think it's important that if a kid really knows that they are totally a boy or totally a girl, and their body doesn't match, they have the options to live as they want. I think people should be educated at a younger age, so they learn to accept queers and trannys and know that there are a lot of us out here.

Q: Is there anything else that we didn't touch on or cover?

A: I wish transitioning was more affordable, insurance-wise, because it's expensive. There should be a special tranny fund so those trannys who can't afford surgery and hormones can still get to transition. It takes a lot of time and energy and money. It would have been harder for me if I didn't have, as I said earlier, a really great partner situation and job situation. If I had been in a minimum wage job with high rent it would have been really hard. Case in point, I have a friend who is going to school, working full-time and struggling to make ends meet. Even though he has benefits and all that kind of stuff, he just can't afford chest surgery. There has got to be some kind of fairy godmother, tranny godmother, father figure, whatever, who could help him. I just wish that somehow it could get easier for low-income people… and not be such a big taboo thing.

| Age 33 | Age 36 | Age 41 |

Stefani Moore works as a writer in the creative services department of a major U.S. corporation. She has her Bachelor's degree in Writing from Pennsylvania State University and her Master's in Secondary Education from Arcadia University. She lives with her son in Bucks County, Pennsylvania.

Through the Looking Glass—and Back Again

When I was a 12-year-old boy I had a dream. Not the Martin Luther King kind of dream. A dream while I was sleeping that shook me to the core, and changed my life.

I drifted off to sleep one night, and dreamt that I was a girl. Not a boy dressed as a girl, but a real live girl with long hair, taffeta skirt, white gloves, black patent leather shoes and a girl's anatomy.

In the dream my family was having a reunion and picnic at our local park. Everyone was there: Aunt Eunice, Uncle Bill and the twins. My brother Jake and sister Ginny ran around between the adults playing tag.

113

My neighbors Pat and Paul were there. It was so real you could smell the hamburgers sizzling on the grill.

And there I was, walking among everyone, wearing a dress. A pretty, Sunday dress just like the ones my sister got to wear to church on Easter Sunday while I stood there strangled by my clip-on tie and blue tweed sports jacket.

The strangest thing about the dream was that no one looked at me funny. No one laughed or joked about Stevie wearing a dress. As I walked around the picnic, everyone—friends, parents, relatives—all treated me as if I truly was a girl, with complete acceptance and love. What a dream! I woke up confused, frightened, and embarrassed. My life has never been quite the same.

It is a pattern that has repeated itself over the years in different forms. At night I never knew if I would dream as a boy, or as a girl. One night I dreamt I was a boy swinging from the trees in Africa with Tarzan and the next night I dreamt I was a girl, making out with Michael Bates, the captain of the football team. For a young teenage boy, the girl dreams were like nightmares.

I never told a soul about my dreams. No one. Not my parents. Not my school chums. Not even my best friend Ricky or my cousin Bart. It was all too confusing. Was I a woman trapped inside a man's body? Were these latent homosexual fears working their way to the surface? Or just my subconscious expressing a suppressed feminine gene through my dreams? I didn't have a clue. So I kept my dreams to myself and prayed they'd go away. They didn't.

In high school when my sister was not around I snuck into her room and tried on her clothes. I tried on her bras and panties and tried to squeeze into her dresses. I did not understand why I was doing it. I just felt compelled. Curious. And after each hurried, terrified exploration of her drawers, I walked away feeling guilty, like there was something horribly wrong with this picture.

When I was 18, I read in the newspaper about tennis pro Renee Richards publishing her book *Second Serve*. That marked the first time I'd ever even heard of a transsexual. Or that it was even possible to have a sex change.

Renee Richards became my secret hero. Right up there with Tarzan and the Fantastic Four. I didn't know if I was a transsexual or not, but for the first time I realized I wasn't alone. I wasn't the only male who dreamt about being a female. The fact that she'd actually changed her sex struck me in the way that lightning must have struck Benjamin Franklin. *The impossible was possible.*

But I was a coward. I was willing clay for my parents, church and school to mold. It wasn't until after I graduated college and was working at our small local newspaper as a reporter, that I spotted a strange personal ad in the back of the *Philadelphia Magazine*:

Behavior Modification Specialist. Ms. Lorena Martin.
P.O. Box 139, Philadelphia, PA 19101

Behavior modification? What the…? I didn't have a clue what it meant. But for some strange reason I connected that tiny little ad with my dreams. So I sat down and wrote a letter to Ms. Lorena Martin. I didn't say much. I didn't tell her about Renee Richards or my dreams, I just introduced myself. A week later I received back a form letter from a professional Dominatrix! At 22 years of age, I'd vaguely heard of BDSM (Bondage Discipline Sadomasochism), knew it had to do with black leather outfits, whips and chains, but that was pretty much the extent of my knowledge of the subject.

In her form letter, Lorena listed a bunch of demands, the crux of which was to write a letter describing my innermost fantasy. I agonized for days over what to do. Did I write back? Did I tell her the truth—that all I wanted to do was find out whether or not I really was a woman? Or maybe just some freak?

She wanted $150 for a "session." I got paid $20 a story at the newspaper. Twenty years ago, $150 was a lot of money for a poor, starving writer. But I did it anyway. This was too important an opportunity to let slip. Heart pounding, I sat down and wrote back a very vague letter, without really describing any sort of fantasy at all. At 22, I still didn't understand, or have the courage to verbalize, what was going on inside me. But still, I felt compelled to reach out to this strange whip wielding woman.

We exchanged several letters, after which Lorena agreed to meet me at a local diner for coffee. Scared to death, I went. Sitting in a booth in the back I found a 44-year-old, curly haired woman with big round glasses, skin as pasty white as Morticia's in the Addams Family, accentuated by a black blouse and jeans.

She hardly looked like a professional Dominatrix. I expected a leather-clad Cat Woman and got a Jewish school teacher.

Lorena was quite friendly, and very chatty. She smiled and laughed a lot. When she continued to probe into what I was looking for—about my fantasies—I still didn't know what to say. I dodged her questions like a matador.

She looked at me almost guiltily. "You're too young. You don't know what you want. And you're single. I don't do single." She paused. "But you are cute." She handed me a business card with her phone number. "Call me."

The card had the name Mistress Lorena Martin, and the same tag line, "Behavior Modification Specialist." I called and made an appointment. "Don't be nervous," she said. "We'll talk... in my dungeon. I'll find out what makes you tick." When I arrived at her row home in Northeast Philadelphia, Lorena met me at the door wearing her Cat Woman, Dominatrix costume, black leather pants, thigh high boots, and a see-through black lace bustier—all covered modestly with a robe as she opened the door.

Leading me upstairs into her spider's web, she took me to a bedroom she'd converted into her dungeon. There were hooks on the ceiling (for hanging more than just plants), a rack, a padded table and a locked cabinet containing instruments of torture. Lorena sat me down, and with her robe wrapped tightly around her, we talked. She was a surprisingly patient, kindly, intelligent woman.

After a while, she stopped talking, looked at her wrist watch and said, "I want you to take off your clothes." I gulped, and nervously began to object. Standing, pulling off her robe, Lorena's attitude flipped like a light switch, from the sympathetic school marm to demanding, leather-clad bitch goddess.

"In my dungeon, you do exactly what I say... *immediately*... or you get the fuck out. Understood?" "Yes," I whispered, unbuttoning my shirt.

"Yes Mistress!" she snapped.

I ended up watching her tie a series of intricate knots, beyond anything I'd ever learned in the boy scouts, around my wrists and ankles. Then watched in horror as she poured hot wax across my nipples, and down my belly to my poor penis.

"Why did you write to me?" she demanded. "You've never described to me your fantasies. Tell me. Tell me now!" Unable to speak the truth, I cried, "This! This is my fantasy. To see you!" Grunting, Lorena put on a rubber glove, doused my crotch with baby oil and masturbated me to a shocking climax. After she was done, and I had dressed, she led me back to her living room where we chatted for an hour, and I left.

Hard to believe as this might sound, she never took any money from me. About a mile down the road I realized her error, and pulled over and called her from a pay phone. She hadn't even realized it herself. She chuckled, and told me it was okay, and we made arrangements to meet again the following week.

So began my relationship with Lorena. I took her out to dinner at a nice restaurant in Center City Philly. We started dating. She said that I was much too young for her, but I could tell that she liked me, and I liked her. I was curious about her lifestyle, and, oddly enough, felt comfortable with her.

As we got to know each other better, Lorena slowly involved me in her world. In small ways at first, like asking me to be her "back up" by sitting in the next room when she had a new client over. And sometimes more. But that isn't what this story is about.

After being with Lorena for three months, one night while we were sitting at her kitchen table, she finally pulled things out of me. She said, "You do all these things I want, but you never talk about what you want. Most men are driving me crazy telling me all of their fantasies. They want their ass beat a thousand times. They want me to screw them with a broomstick. Tie them upside down from my chandelier. But you. All but you."

"I just don't think about things like that," I shrugged. Lorena looked at me like I was hiding something. "Everyone has fantasies. I know you. You're keeping something from me, I can tell. You don't have to be afraid. You can tell me. Look at all the things I tell you! I tell you everything!"

Did I dare? "Well, there is one thing," I found myself saying. Oh no.

"I knew it," she grinned. "Go on. Tell me." I winced and found my heart racing. "I've never told anyone this before..." "Well, what is it then?" How did I tell her? How did I admit to her something that I had a hard time admitting to myself?

"If you don't tell me, you know me, I'll paddle it out of you."

"All my life I've had these dreams," I blurted out.

"What kind of dreams?" Lorena asked with genuine interest. "Tell me everything." "W-w-well," I stammered, and told her about the first dream I'd had when I was 12 years old, of being at a family picnic dressed like a girl.

"And you still have dreams like this? That you're dressed as a woman?"

"It's not only that I'm dressed as a woman," I said helplessly, "*I am a woman!* Do you have dreams that you're a man?"

"No, can't say that I do." So this wasn't a common phenomenon. There was something wrong with me. I was sick.

"So that's it?"

"Yes. I've always been so afraid to tell anyone…"

"So that's your fantasy? You want to dress like a woman?" "I don't know," I said red faced. "I guess I've always wondered what it would be like… to be the girl in my dreams. But I'm afraid. Afraid I might like it." I squinted and looked at her, expecting her to laugh at me. "So what do you think?"

Lorena grinned. "I think we need to go shopping."

For me, that's how it all began. The following weekend Lorena took me to a women's boutique across the bridge in New Jersey. I thought I would die when she started holding dresses up against me right in the middle of the store—and I pretty much did die a thousand deaths when she threw me into a changing booth and started feeding me dresses to try on—even going so far as to bring a grinning saleswoman into the booth with her to get my measurements. Ah well, such is the life of a professsional Dominatrix's boy toy—or a Jewish woman's boyfriend (take your pick).

It's a day I'll never forget because I bought my first little black dress. We went home and Lorena sat me down, did my makeup and put one of her long brunette wigs on me. I put on my new dress and a pair of 3-inch open-toed pumps—and took my first steps through the looking glass.

Lorena made me wait until I was fully made up before opening her closet door and letting me see my full reflection. "I want you to get the full effect," she said. It is a moment I will never forget. I felt like I was seeing my Self for the first time. Instead of putting on women's clothes, I felt like I had stripped something away to reveal my soul within. There, staring back at me in the mirror was my twin sister. My heart cracked open, and a phoenix emerged. Like the beautiful mythological Greek Narcissus, I fell in love with my image and wanted to spend the rest of the day staring at myself.

Lorena had other plans. It would therefore be my first trip out of the house dressed fully as a woman. So I got fully dressed and came out of the closet all in one day.

I owe her a world of thanks. As the first person I ever opened up to, she was accepting and supportive. She taught me how to do my makeup. She allowed me to dress as a woman whenever I felt like it. She helped me accumulate a wardrobe, and she also told me about a TV/TS support group in the Philadelphia area called Renaissance.

We went to one of their meetings together. It was incredibly liberating. There, inside an office building, were over 75 transgendered people of every age, shape, size and denomination. There were pre-ops sitting in a discussion group talking about hormone therapy. There was a rap session for post-ops discussing assimilating into society. There was a woman leading a demonstration on electrolysis.

My relationship with Lorena lasted about a year. I really wasn't into kink. I'm not a sadist or a masochist. Lorena loved putting me into strict bondage, paddling my ass every time I made an error, and used me as her guinea pig every time she bought a new sex toy. It was a fun ride, but in the end, I came to the conclusion that I just wanted a "normal" relationship with someone. Lorena and I never had sexual intercourse. She didn't care for it. She could be a sweetheart, and was very kind to me, but at her core she admitted she was a sadist and got off on inflicting pain. The relationship was not destined to last forever, and it didn't. Twenty years later, Lorena and I are still friends, and she loves to remind me, "I am the one who made you who you are today." She certainly opened the door.

Through Renaissance, I discovered the alternative lifestyle community in New Hope, PA. The gay bars there (the Prelude, the Cartwheel and the Raven) held regular drag shows that drew huge crowds of not only gay men and lesbians, but also cross-dressers, drag queens and the transgendered community. Lorena and I went to some of the shows together. "Don't you dare come here alone," she said firmly as we drove home one night.

Bad girl that I am, I could not stay away. One night I slipped up to New Hope on my own to watch the drag show, and saw a stunningly beautiful woman in the corner chatting with a group of friends. She had the facial features of a model, a willowy figure, was about 5'9", had toffee colored skin and was dressed fashionably in a little black dress with cutouts that revealed her skin down the sides. It was one of the few times I've ever experienced that rare sensation of "love at first sight." So much so, that I tapped a man on the shoulder in the crowd, pointed at the woman, and asked, "Who is that?" The guy looked in the direction I pointed and said, "That's Renee Russo, the prettiest boy in New Hope." Boy? *That's a boy?*

Renee was surrounded by admiring friends, so I did not approach her, but a month later I went back again, this time dressed as a man with the sole purpose of hopefully running into this beautiful creature.

Eventually our paths crossed, and when they did, once more the entire path of my life changed. I saw Renee sitting alone at the back bar in the Cartwheel, and sat next to her. She looked at me and smiled, I smiled back, and the rest was history. We started chatting, and never stopped chatting for six years. I went home with Renee that night, made love to her, and fell completely and utterly head over heels in love. In the morning I woke up before she did as I had to get to work. Not wanting to wake her, but also wanting to leave her some sort of a message, all I could find was her purse. I took her lipstick and wrote my name and phone number across her bathroom mirror. Would she call? All day at the newsroom I replayed the night before over and over in my mind. Renee was a pre-op transsexual, with a slender body, small hormone-induced breasts, and a shrunken penis. For the first time in a year I'd actually made love to someone. For the first time in a long time I'd actually felt masculine. And enjoyed it. Anything to be next to Renee.

She called! Around lunch time she called, told me she'd had a wonderful time, and we made plans to go out to dinner that weekend.

Thus ended my relationship with Lorena. I didn't have to tell her I met Renee. All I had to do was tell her I'd been to New Hope without her, and when she wanted to put me over her knee and use a hair brush on me, I said, "No more." I packed what things I had at her place. We argued viciously over a pair of women's shoes (of all things), and sadly, ended on bad terms. Fortunately, years later I called Lorena, and we patched things up, and have been able to remain friends ever since.

On my first date with Renee we went to a restaurant in New Jersey called Wildflowers. It was a family place, and I found it utterly amazing how flawlessly Renee passed as a woman. No one would have had the slightest clue that she was actually a transsexual. She was gorgeous, her hair done stylishly, nails done in a French manicure, and her clothes impeccable.

As we chatted over dinner I learned Renee worked at the restaurant in the Cartwheel as the hostess. She also traveled all over the country doing drag shows. She was exactly my age, and she'd been living as a woman full-time since her Marine drill sergeant father threw her out of the house in Chicago at age 17.

Renee had lived all over the country, from Hollywood to New England to Florida. She'd also worked as a showgirl in Las Vegas and did the LaCage show in Manhattan and Atlantic City. Some of her show friends had invited her to perform in New Hope, and there she had remained till our paths crossed.

From that moment on, Renee and I were inseparable. Three months later we moved her out of her apartment in New Hope into the farmhouse I'd bought in Bucks County, PA.

Renee knew about my cross-dressing, and hated it. Right from the start she told me, "Only one of us is going to wear dresses in this relationship—and it's going to be me." We had a blowout fight about it—which Renee won by humiliating me for days by calling me "Stefani" when I was dressed as a boy in front of my straight friends. I was so mortified and embarrassed, I took all of my women's clothes, makeup, jewelry, everything—packed them up in hefty bags and dropped them all in the trash.

"You will never hear me talk about this subject again," I said. And I didn't. For six years.

Renee had wanted me to be the man in the relationship, and unlike Lorena, Renee didn't need to use a paddle to get her way. I chalk it up to love. I would have done anything for Renee. And I did. I put aside my dreams.

Among the first big events in our relationship, was Renee's running for Miss Gay Pennsylvania. It was the first time they were holding the pageant in Pennsylvania, and Renee wanted to win. She did too. It was a fierce competition among drag queens and transsexuals from all over the state— but Renee pulled it off. And was quite proud of the fact that she would always be remembered as the first Miss Gay Pennsylvania.

I followed her entourage to Texas where Renee competed in the Miss Gay America finals. She didn't win Miss Gay America, but she was chosen among the Top 10, and got to compete in the prestigious finals with the best of the best.

Those were thrilling times. The next year Renee competed for Miss New Jersey and won, and the year after that, she flew to Detroit to win the Miss Gay Michigan pageant. All so she could get back to the finals and hopefully become Miss Gay America. She never did win the crown she coveted, but she got close, and was respected in the industry as a true professional.

During the years I lived with Renee, my son from a three-month relationship I'd had with a woman before I met Lorena, came to live with Renee and me. He had just turned five and started school. My son, Jake, never had a clue that Renee was anything other than she appeared to be, an attractive woman. For Renee, our relationship was a dream come true. As a transsexual she was living with a man who adored her, and she was helping to raise his son. Renee might have had the adulation of her fans, but I gave her something she never had—a family. We went on vacations to the beach and Disney World together. We did everything your typical family did, and Renee absolutely loved it.

At the same time I quit the newspaper and went to work for my family's business, where my income jumped dramatically. So we lived well. I drove a Porsche, gave Renee a handful of credit cards and told her to buy whatever she needed. Life was good. Until reality struck. Hard.

One morning when Renee and I woke, I noticed the bed sheets were soaked. Renee had been sweating profusely as she slept. When I asked her what was wrong, she shrugged it off and said, "It happens sometimes."

I felt a pang of fear, my thoughts going to the articles I'd read about AIDS symptoms, one of which was night sweats. When I'd been with Lorena, even though we'd always practiced safe sex, I'd gotten nervous about her having been active with her male submissives and got myself tested. It was a gut-wrenching experience as you had to wait a week for the results. Thankfully, they'd been negative.

With Renee we'd practiced safe sex the first two months of our relationship, but then had discarded our condoms. For all the revealing costumes Renee wore on stage she was extremely conservative sexually. Because of the hormones she was on, she really didn't have much of a sex drive.

But what she did have—was a partner before me named Bruce. A man that had turned out to be as bad as they come, a drug addicted alcoholic, currently serving time in Graterford Prison for armed robbery.

After Renee's night sweats, I went back to the clinic and got tested again. After a week, I went back for the results. The woman at the desk looked at me sadly. "Your results came back positive." She recommended various doctors, but this was back in the 1990's when there were no medicines. All they had was AZT. AIDS was a death sentence. I walked outside of the clinic, and cried.

When I got home and told Renee the news, she was shocked. "You need to get tested too," I said. She did, and we learned she was positive as well. Her reaction was anger. She went berserk, telling me it was my fault.

"Look Renee," I said, "there's no point in either of us blaming one another. Who gave it to whom, doesn't make a difference now. We just have to deal with it." We had to stay together. And we did. Until Renee died of pneumonia. Later, we would learn that Bruce was in jail with AIDS. And he would die of it there.

When I told Jake that Renee had died, he began to cry. He looked up at me through his tears and said, "Who's going to take care of us now?" Which was understandable. While I was working, Renee had been the one that had helped him with his schoolwork, taken care of the house, and fed us.

Jake's mother had married and had another child. We were on our own. He was just eight years old, and I was 29. I wondered if I'd live to see him graduate high school.

After Renee's death, I went into a deep depression. If it weren't for Jake I might have wanted to commit suicide. I'd watched Renee's bright spirit slowly fade and wither. And I knew the same fate awaited me.

With my own t-cells diminishing, thinking I probably had about five years left to live, I made some drastic changes in my life. I quit my family's business, which I'd never really enjoyed (only doing it for the money) and went back to college to get my Master's degree in Education. I figured I'd spend my final years sharing my passion for writing and literature with students.

I sold my portion of the business I'd accumulated, giving me enough money to survive without working for a couple of years, during which time I could go to school. Why work, when the end appeared in sight?

And then I did something else. I started dressing like a woman again. With Renee gone, my dreams came back. I found myself cross-dressing within months of her funeral.

And a year after her death, I found myself sitting in a doctor's office dressed as a woman, telling him I wanted to have a sex change. Did I? I wasn't really sure. But I knew from Renee's transgendered friends, that if I walked into this particular doctor's office dressed as a girl, and told him I wanted to be a woman—he'd prescribe hormones. Which he did. Immediately.

I figured if I only had a few years to live, I wanted to live them as a woman. And I'd learned enough from Renee to know that if you wanted to pass, you had to get on premarin and spiro. I got my ears pierced. Grew my hair long. Plucked my eyebrows, shaved my legs, and say hey babe, I say hey honey, I began my walk on the wild side.

My friends and family noticed the changes, and were shocked. But I didn't care. There is something about knowing this year might be your last that inspires you to live out your days the way you want to. Not the way society says you must. This was my life. And I'd spend what I had left living the way I chose. And the desire to live out my days as a female was overpowering. Strong enough to make me start giving myself weekly estradiol valerate injections and undergo five years of Chinese torture called electrolysis.

Around the same time Jake, at 11 years old, came home from school one day, and said, "Megan says that Renee was a man." Uh-oh. My neighbors knew the truth about Renee. People were talking. He still seemed so young. I'd been tip-toeing around him—hiding, dressing on the weekends when he was off at his mother's house. The time had come to talk. Better for me to tell him than the kids at the bus stop.

"Renee was born a man," I said.

He looked perplexed. "Then why did she dress like a girl?"

"She looked pretty as a girl, didn't she? You thought she was a girl, right?"

"Well, yeah," he said.

"That's just who Renee was. She wanted to live that way, and she did. Does that make you feel any less toward her? Do you still love her?"

He thought about it for a minute, and said, rather thoughtfully for an 11-year-old, "Yes. It doesn't change a thing." Then my son looked up at me, and surprised me by asking, "Are you going to become a girl?" What better opening. "Yes. Sort of." Then he floored me by motioning to my crotch and asking, "Are you going to change your…?"

My 11-year-old son knew about sex changes? And by the way he said it, I knew he thought Renee had gone through SRS. No reason to change that thought.

"I don't know," I answered truthfully. And I didn't. I knew I wanted to live as a woman, to let this side of myself shine forth, but I really didn't know if I could make the final cut. "Does this bother you?"

Jake shook his head no. And surprised me again, by saying, "I don't care what you wear. Just don't make me look bad in front of my friends." All of which seemed quite reasonable. And paved the way for me to stop hiding in my own house. I respected my son's wishes and toned it down in front of his friends.

As he got older, there were times when he might be having friends over to watch a DVD, and I was going out to some function in a dress. Jake would shove me out the front door, as his friends came in the back door. We joked and laughed about it. But it was never a problem between us.

As Jake got older things evolved. One day when Jake was in his teens I asked him, "Do you think your friends know about me?"

"How could they not?!" he cried. "You've got a rack of women's shoes behind your door. Pictures of yourself as a girl all over the place. Makeup all over the bathroom."

"Do your friends ever say anything?"

"No. But they know."

As did my neighbors and eventually everyone else in my life, including Jake's mother, Penny. She said to Jake, "I think your father is getting weird. You need to come live with me." Jake said, "No. It's all right mom. I want to stay here." My friends and neighbors all came to accept the changes in me (though my family never did).

During this period, I received a phone call from one of Renee's friends, a very handsome black man named Keith. He called and asked me out on a dinner date! I was floored, and didn't know how to respond. I hadn't dated at all. And being HIV+, wasn't sure I should.

I said to Keith, "Do you know how Renee died?"

"I heard it was pneumonia," he said slowly. "Did she have…?"

"Yes," I said filling in the blank. "She had AIDS."

"Do you have...?"

"Yes, I'm HIV+," I replied. "Still want to go out with me?"

Keith thought about it for a moment, and said, "Yes, I do. I appreciate you being honest with me. But it doesn't matter. I'd still like you to come by for dinner." I was lonely and so I did. When I got to Keith's house in Trenton, I was floored. The entire downstairs was filled with candles. There was a bottle of champagne cooling by the dinner table that was set with a fresh arrangement of flowers. And he was cooking steak and lobster.

We ate and chatted. I learned Keith worked with mentally handicapped adults, helping mainstream them into society. Finding them housing and jobs. He had majored in Theater at Temple University and had a great sense of humor and an infectious laugh. For the first time since Renee died I found myself relaxing.

And for the first time in my life I felt what it was like to be chased by a man that not only liked me… he lusted for me. Before the night was through we ended up in Keith's bed. He was an incredible lover. Handsome. Gentle. Well-built… especially where it counted!

And I was a bit of a basket case. Confused by my attraction to Keith. Feeling guilty for being "untrue" to Renee. And completely incapable of any male sort of response. Keith didn't care. He swept me up in his arms. My heart quickened as he climbed on top of me. His body felt so hard…

"You have to use a condom!" I bleated.

"Don't worry," he whispered. "I will."

We made love, and I was overcome by the sensation that it *takes a real man to make you feel like a real woman.*

Thus began a five year relationship. Keith was unlike any partner I'd ever had. He made me feel like an equal partner. We quickly became not only lovers, but best friends. Talking constantly, several times a day.

We lived close enough to see each other whenever we wanted, and began spending all our weekends together. Jake spent weekends with his mother—so Keith and I spent them together, rotating back and forth between our respective houses. Each of us maintaining our own space. But sharing everything else. Life with Keith was like living the Sade song, "No Ordinary Love." Keith truly brightened every day with his sweet smile.

At first I was a reluctant lover. The more I liked him, the more I feared I could hurt him by infecting him with the "gay plague." Keith never worried. And quite stupidly said to me one night when he was out of condoms, "I'm going to catch it sooner or later. It might as well be from you."

"You're an asshole!" I told him angrily. And refused to make love. One of the things I am proudest about—is the fact that I made Keith get tested year after year—and he always came up negative. All of which helped me to finally relax, and eventually enjoy being with him. He was incredible.

Like with Renee, Jake and I formed our own little alternative nuclear family with Keith. We went to the beach together. Keith taught Jake how to golf. We ate several nights a week together as a family. Embarrassing as it is to admit, Keith was a much better cook. He took over my kitchen, or threw huge parties at his home in Mill Hill, entertaining the high society of New Hope, and did all the cooking himself. To use one of his phrases, Keith was *big fun*.

Keith was also gay. He didn't understand why I was on hormones, and hated the fact that they killed my sex drive. But I didn't care. Being HIV+, not being able to have erections was a good thing. At times I felt like my penis was like a dangerous pistol. And the hormones took the bullets out of the gun.

My conservative, religious family was horrified by what I was doing with my body—and now dating a black man? My parents stopped me at their threshold like I had turned into a vampire, and forbade me to enter their house.

"Put your hair in a ponytail. Take out the earrings. And wash the makeup off your face," my father said to me on the phone. "We are inviting *our son* over to dinner. We don't know who that other person is. And we don't care to know."

Eventually my family softened regarding Keith, and came to like him. My mother even said to me, "We could accept it if you were gay. If you met a nice doctor or lawyer and settled down. *But you!* You're way beyond gay!"

Although my family threatened to throw me out, they never stopped loving me. They expressed their opinions—and held nothing back. Nor did I. We went toe to toe. They armed with their Bibles, spouting verses from the Old Testament, along with plenty of fire and brimstone.

I battled back with common sense, charity, and love. I told my parents, "The gay and gender community is no different than your church community. They support and take care of each other. Their relationships are based on *love*. The only real difference between the alternative community and the religious community is that you're a lot more self-righteous. What do you think goes on in New Hope? That it's Sodom and Gomorrah? What do you think we do when we have dinner parties? Do you think they're orgies? If there is anything perverted going on—it's going on in your head! What gives you the right to even think about my sexuality? Do I look inside your bedroom door? Do you look in my brother's and sister's bed?"

"Stop!" my mother yelled at me, putting her hands over her ears. "*Stop making sense!*" My parents hated arguing with me. So we agreed on a truce. We adopted the Clinton "don't ask, don't tell policy," and things went back to the more peaceful way they used to be.

In 1995 the medical community came out with the new HIV medicines that we have today. They called it the "triple cocktail." My t-cells had slipped over the years from the normal range down perilously close to the danger zone. But the new medicines changed everything. In time my t-cells starting going up. The death sentence had been lifted.

Through it all, I rarely had so much as a cold. Since 1990 I've been living at death's door, and yet ironically, I have the constitution of a steel drum and have rarely been sick at all.

Sensing a ray of hope for the first time in years, I decided to use some of the money I'd put away from the sale of my part of our family's business to have some plastic surgery on my face to make it more feminine. The hormones helped, but I still had certain masculine features like my Adam's apple that I wanted to get rid of. I made an appointment with a local, well-known plastic surgeon in Philadelphia—and came away crushed. During our consultation, the doctor looked at my medical history, which I'd been quite honest about, and looked at me and said, "I wouldn't touch you with a 10-foot pole." He said he was sorry, but that he couldn't help me.

Not ready to give up, I explored the internet, and learned about a TG-friendly doctor in San Francisco named Dr. Douglas Ousterhout. The mystical "Dr. O." The Wizard of Oz among transsexuals that magically turned boys into girls. He was renowned in transgendered circles as the best facial plastic surgeon in the country. He'd literally written the medical textbook on "Facial Feminization."

I wrote to Dr. O's office, and I exchanged several letters with his darling assistant Mira, who asked me to take several pictures of my face from all different angles. I did, and received Dr. O's recommendations, which included rhinoplasty (a nose job), contouring of my jaw, and a trachea shave—all of which I agreed to, and would cost me $15,000 and a week in the Davies Medical Center.

During the course of our communication, I let Dr. O. know that I was HIV+ and held my breath. He thanked me for my honesty, and said that any intelligent, responsible physician put procedures into place to protect himself and his staff from people who could be HIV+ and weren't as up-front about it. So it would not be a problem. I literally did a dance with joy! I was off to see the Wizard!

When I finally made it out to Davies Medical Center I was blown away by Mira's hospitality and Dr. O's professionalism. The surgery was rough. When I woke up, I found myself wound in bandages like a mummy, my long hair sticking out at wild angles, tubes sticking into my arm… and a catheter in my penis!

Still doped up, I forced my body out of bed and over to a mirror. My eyes blinked. Was that me!? My normally long face was round and swollen. What little skin I could see around my eyes was black and blue. The bandages crisscrossed over my nose made me look like I'd been beaten with a baseball bat. I couldn't even recognize myself! I staggered back to bed, and cried.

While I was still out of it, my parents called! Half in a daze, I listened to my frightened father ranting, "Keith told us what you are doing! He gave us the number of the hospital—but they don't have anyone registered under your name. When I told them where you lived in Pennsylvania, they told me I must be looking for *Stefani!* Why didn't you tell us you were going off to have a *sex change!?*"

"Mmm… maybe because I didn't," I said my mouth feeling full of cotton balls. "All I did was get a nose job. I'll be home in a week."

"You had my nose!" my father yelled. "You had the Martin nose! What was wrong with your nose?!"

I cried for the next several days, terrified that I wouldn't recognize myself when the bandages came off. The absolute worst was when Dr. O. used a pair of pliers to pull the packing from my nostril. I almost did a back flip out of his chair. And then to go through it a second time!

I was one sorry tranny for a few weeks, with a swollen face and two black eyes, but when finally everything healed, I was delighted with the results! No more Adam's apple. Good-bye to all my turtle necks, scarves and chokers! Woohoo! And now I had a cute little pug nose, just like my sister's. I felt like one of the Bond girls—only I was one of the Wizard of O's girls.

By the end of the summer I'd healed and went back to finish my Master's and do my student teaching at a rough urban school outside of Philadelphia. I taught Shakespeare to gifted students, had a group of middle track seniors, the honors freshmen, and two classes of low track freshmen from the ghetto.

Amazingly, even though my hair was all the way down my back and I wore earrings and an armload of bracelets (and I was 5'11" and only 140 pounds) the other teachers and smarter kids didn't have a clue as to the fact that I was transgendered. It was the drug dealers, gang members and so-called "mental defectives" in my two lower track classes that knew everything about me.

"Hey, Mr. Martin, were you out in a pink dress last Saturday night? Benny said he saw you leaving your house in a pink dress," one kid cat-called right in the middle of class. Actually I'd been out in a black dress. Another time, *Do you have a black boyfriend?* And one day while walking through the halls, I overheard two black girls giggling behind me. "Oh, he's a *she* all right." All of which left me red-faced as a steamed crab. I didn't want to discuss my personal life in front of the students, and didn't. I dodged their questions and stuck to the lessons.

"Hey, Mr. Martin, what does that rainbow bumper sticker on your car mean? *Is that the gay flag?*"

"Why Greg," I shot back at the student, whose name was Gregory Peck, and oddly enough, had never even heard of the actor of the same name who starred in *To Kill A Mockingbird*. "Are you trying to tell us that you are gay, Greg? What? Are you trying to ask me to the prom Greg? Is that what this is all about?"

The students in the class all turned to look at Greg and laugh. Shutting him up. Temporarily.

Although I loved 90% of the students and the experience was incredibly rewarding, at the same time I realized, on hormones as I was, and all that I'd gone through, I wasn't ready for prime time. Or, they weren't ready for me. Whichever.

When I finished my Master's program, a major corporation offered me a writing job, and I snapped it up. I began working the Creative Services Department of a huge newsroom style office of 150 people. I was one among 10 writers and 10 artists. No one cared about my long hair, bracelets, plucked eyebrows or earrings. Interestingly, some people in the building weren't sure if I was a man or a woman. I got called "ma'am" or "miss" a lot, and just smiled in return.

My boss, the head of the copy department later told me, "When I interviewed you, I liked you, but I wasn't sure about the way you looked, so I went to Tom, the President, and asked him what to do. Tom asked if I thought you could do the work. I said yes, but was concerned because you didn't exactly look like *corporate America*. He told me as long as you could write, he didn't give a damn what you looked like. So I hired you." So I had a job, which I needed, because it was now past the year 2002 and, miraculously, I was still alive. And needed to get back to work.

During my years with Keith, I met a man through the internet named John. He was a retired doctor in his 70's who lived on the West Coast and had been transgendered himself when he was younger. We struck up a friendship, and he quickly became my greatest supporter and confidant when it came to my transition.

We met and he generously offered to help me with any surgeries I desired. If anything John felt that I was moving too slowly. If you're going to go through the full change, you should do it now while you're still young and you can enjoy life."

None of which Keith liked hearing.

"Your transition is moving at glacial speed," John commented when we chatted on the phone.

True, I'd been on hormones for five years now. John warned me that if I waited too long to have reassignment surgery, the anti-testosterones I was taking would reduce what little I had left of my penis to the point there would be nothing to work with to create a vagina.

John had one arm pulling me in one direction and Keith had my other arm pulling me the opposite way.

In the summer of 2002, when Keith and I went off to spend a week vacation in Provincetown, MA, I spent the entire time as a woman. He looked at me, torn. He loved me, but I had all but killed the man he loved.

One night as we sat in the Lobster Pot eating seafood, he looked at me and said, "The only thing still masculine about you... is your penis. And that doesn't even work."

We had a wonderful life together, but ultimately Keith was a gay man—and I'd become a woman. Even when I went out dressed in male clothes, people still thought I was a woman. Although Keith had taken it in stride for years, and even applauded me at times, he was finally reaching the end of his limits.

Shortly after Provincetown, I flew out to Portland to spend a week with my mentor, John. Although I was nervous about the airport security hassling me because of my male I.D., no one said a thing. After the ticket person handed me back my I.D., a baggage handler looked at me and said, "Can I take your bag *Miss*?"

My fear melted away. I could do this.

As I sat on the plane beside a woman passenger, she chatting about her children and I about Jake, suddenly she looked at me and said, "So I guess your son is home with his father?" I couldn't help but smile. The woman had no idea that *I* was the father. I took it for granted that people saw me for what I was, a transsexual. But after six years of hormones and a trip to Oz, I was passing well. I probably should have felt ecstatic, and I did in a way, but I also felt like something was wrong. *I wasn't a woman.* Not a genetic female like the one I was chatting with. And was I fooling not only her, but also myself into thinking I could ever hope to mimic her chromosomes?

While I was visiting John, he took me to visit the office of the renowned gender reassignment surgeon in Portland, Dr. Toby Meltzer. According to John, who had been a respected physician himself, Meltzer was the best.

"If you ever decide to move your transition out of neutral," he said as we entered the office, "I want you to go to Toby."

Insane as it sounds, even though I was living as a woman, I'd never really given gender reassignment surgery serious thought. If anything, I avoided thinking about it. Especially when they started describing the operation. Inverting the penis. Using the testicles to create labia. The electrolysis you had to undergo to get rid of the pubic hair on your penis. *Ouch!*

Dr. Meltzer wasn't in, which disappointed John, but in a way I was relieved. We'd taken a chance and just walked in unannounced, and did get to meet his staff, who loaded us up with paperwork and brochures.

When I returned from Portland, Keith picked me up at the Philadelphia airport. As he drove me home, he told me he'd had enough. The trip to Portland, where he knew John was encouraging me to go through reassignment surgery, was the last straw for Keith. It was over. Even though I cried and told him I didn't want the operation, Keith wasn't listening. It was time for him to move on, and he was right.

I continued to work as a writer and dress androgynously at work, and spend all my free time as a woman. After Keith, I bounced around from relationship to relationship with men that could best be described as "tranny chasers." Men lined up to ask me out on dates, all with only one thought in mind; trying to get me drunk enough to go home to bed—or better yet, out to their car to blow them.

I began to develop a definite distaste for men. They all wanted to get into my panties—but not one of them had the guts to take me home to meet his parents or his friends. It's amazing how many macho "straight" men, especially married ones, have a secret fantasy about doing a 'chick with a dick.' They're really quite the charmers.

One night at the Silver Swan in Manhattan, I looked at a 40-something married man who was hitting on me hard, and said to him, "You're married. You're cheating on your wife. Why would I trust a man like you? I don't even like you. But I do like your wife. And I'm going to do her a favor. I'm HIV+. If I let you in my panties, you'd be taking that home to her. And I don't think that's fair to her."

The man turned white as a tablecloth and nearly dove through the front plate glass window of the famous German restaurant and TG hangout in his hurry to run away.

At work, I was teamed with an attractive, straight, conservative, married woman named Joan. Good Catholic girl that she was, Joan sang in the church choir, was a regular PTA mom to her two daughters, and a devoted wife to her macho, pea-brained husband.

Spending eight hours a day working side by side, and going to lunch every day together, Joan and I became best friends. Even though our lives were at opposite ends of the social spectrum—she the married church lady, I the transgendered slut—we had mutual respect in one another's work ethic and ability.

We told each other everything. I told her about my dates from hell. And she told me how she'd been a virgin when she'd married her husband, and how for the past 16 years their sex life had consisted of his coming either prematurely on her belly, or after about five seconds of being inside her. Poor girl!

After a year of working together, and not only talking all day at work, but all evening on the phone as well… and then joining the YMCA together… and starting to exercise after work together… suddenly one day after lunch Joan leaned over in my car and kissed me full on the lips. Shocked, I pushed her away.

Tears glistened in her eyes immediately. "You're rejecting me too!"

"You're married!" I cried. Besides, I like *men*. Or at least I thought I did.

That one little kiss marked a major turning point in my life. The next day I did not push Joan away. We spent half our lunch break in the park by our office building necking like two teenagers. And spent the next year, holding hands and kissing, constantly. Everywhere. In the back seat of her SUV. Or under the stairwell in the office. Or hidden in the pines in the park. With Joan married, and me pickled on hormones, our physical options were limited, which made for a great romantic relationship.

Ultimately Joan and I did not go very far, but she opened a new window in my mind. What was I doing with my life? I was sick of men. But I couldn't be with women. What woman would want me?

Joan kept pushing me to see a counselor, and although I resisted at first, eventually I agreed. I'd been to several over the years, and most seemed like crackpots, like they should have been the ones laying on the padded couch.

Eventually I found the right therapist, a wonderful older woman named Heidi. Whereas most counselors I'd been to seemed to spend 50 of the 60 minutes lecturing, Heidi listened. She asked perceptive questions, and then

I got to listen to my *honest* response. The first couple of sessions I cried. *What was I doing with my life?* I wasn't so much a woman, as a failed man.

In the end, I decided to get off hormones. It was like trying to kick a heroin addiction. I liked my life as a transsexual. I liked the attention. I liked not having a sex drive. I liked the added emotions, and feared I'd turn into some sort of grizzly bear that drank beer, belched and scratched its belly.

After eight years on hormones, my New Year's resolution for 2005 was to stay off hormones, and I have. Of course I still go out dressed as a woman. But I no longer experience an all-encompassing and over-powering urge to dress and live as a woman. I have come to learn that on the gender scale, I fit somewhere in the middle. I'll always be a mix of masculine and feminine.

What I wear just doesn't seem to matter so much today. They're just clothes, for God's sake. I am who I am, from the inside out—not from the outside in.

Age 2 ½   Age 38

Grady Challis is a performer, visual artist and home economist who lives with a pair of frisky dogs, some ukuleles, and a landslide of unfinished craft projects. Happy with his lot in life, he is most likely to be found somewhere quiet, strumming happy old-time tunes, as something delicious bakes in the oven.

I Left My Breasts in San Francisco

I am nine years old, and I am helping my grandmother cook breakfast in the kitchen. We are the only ones awake. Following that 1950's sitcom-couple twin-bed-mandate to an extreme, my grandparents sleep in separate rooms, and my grandfather will not make his morning appearance until he is summoned to breakfast. This is a brand of deference—he knows his presence in the midst of our cooking would make us feel pressured and uncomfortable. He is a man I idolize, and who reciprocates my reverence with a vague blanket of adoration, but no definite use for me since I'm a girl.

My grandmother is teaching me to fry bacon, and I am awkwardly holding a large skillet full of fatty meat in half an inch of boiling grease. As the bacon cooks, pieces of the hot fat spit and hiss, avenging the anguish of the pan by burning my hands. I pull my sweatshirt sleeves over them while protesting to my grandmother, who tells me in a sweet, detached voice that someday I'm going to have a husband of my own who will want me to cook bacon for him every morning, so I'm better off getting used to it now.

I am seventeen, and I am entering my senior year of high school. My hair hangs long over my breasts. I am sure of nothing in this world except that I am fat, and ugly, and will never be sexy. Amy is a worldly twenty-four, a waitress at a dumpy bar near the college, and she fucks every pretty girl. She is renowned for breaking up the most solidly heterosexual relationships and she does not hit on girls lightly. She flirts with stabbing eyes, missiles painted with come-ons, and free pitchers of beer—landmines in the path of any straight girl who happens to wander in without her boyfriend. Right this moment I'm worrying that I've spread my legs too easily to keep her attention long. Her dirty blonde hair is thick and looks rough, but feels soft, rubbing the tops of my thighs with the motions of her head.

This doesn't feel anything like it has before, when boyfriends headed south on me, returning shortly with grins that said they'd stamped their passports and were now world travelers. Compared to this, they hadn't even driven to Canada, much less ventured overseas. I'm trying to remember everything she's doing, using the experience as a CliffsNotes for the inevitable moment of reciprocation. In my body, the shame and fear of this is competing with how unfuckingbelieveablyjesuschristgod-DAMN good it feels, and I will myself to hurry up and come before the fear and the guilt win out over what feels like it just might be my Very First Orgasm. It's knotting my stomach, it's hot, maybe it's hot because it is terrifying, and it's all feeling more and more certain to be my future than my impending high school graduation is. I wonder if I'm bisexual —a word that seems to promise I may finally have a chance at being sexually popular. I wonder if I'm a lesbian, and wish it didn't sound quite so much like something a sailor could catch on shore leave.

I am twenty, and I am dating Melissa, a teacher from my college. Tonight we are lying awake in bed, late, arguing over the religious upbringing of our future children, although they are not yet a twinkle in their sperm donor's eye this night.

I'm not a girly girl anymore, but I'm not a butch yet, either. I'm in the middle—the kind of lesbian that stays a lesbian, never a dyke. Who by the time she is thirty-five will have a lumpy set of coffee mugs in her cupboard that she made in pottery class, and in her window—intertwined against a lavender background—two women's symbols in a stained glass suncatcher.

By now, my sex with women has developed a more practiced, harder edge. We thumb through our Pat Califia stories, but we hide the books under the mattress when we have company. Melissa regularly compares our bodies, and I have become familiar with the slight but insistent shifts that time will manifest in my body when I am her age, a decade from now. As we argue, I find the sight of our four breasts lined up above the folded blanket rather sweet. I silence her next point with my mouth on her body.

I am twenty-three, and I am an inadvertent, part-time boy. For the next couple of years my femaleness will be irregularly invisible. This will delight, anger and frighten me. This afternoon, I am at my mom's sixtieth birthday party. One of the male guests is slapping me on the back with a liver-spotted hand, making jokes about how incompetent women drivers are as he jerks a thumb at his date, who sits on the sofa with a cup of punch, a stiffly sprayed hairdo, and firmly crossed ankles. Thanks to my grandmother's Sunday morning lessons, I'm a good Southern girl, meaning that while I might have sex with other girls, I will never be rude to a guest. So I smile politely, and say nothing. He peers at my mom through his heavily-lined bifocals, adjusts the lapel on his burgundy polyester blazer, tells my mom what a nice son she has. She looks pained, and I feel it. I know how she hates people knowing I'm a dyke, how uncomfortable she is with the attention I get from them, how they stare at my shorn head and combat boots when we go to the mall. I don't yet know that she will stretch to meet me in future years, how she will speak of her love and pride for me until it's one of the surest things in my world. I don't yet know how much closer we will become, how I will rely on her. All I can see right now is that her discomfort will not be mitigated when someone acknowledges and approves of me as her son.

I am a slight, crew-cutted girl who has worked to master the art of the swagger, who attracts misplaced femmes with hungry eyes and lips glossed with strawberry-flavored, oh-so innocent sexiness. I sleep with them, and then ignore them, and then sleep with them again, imitating the standoffish attitude flecked with the promise of vulnerability that worked for those bad boys in after-school specials. Out of their sight, I read John Preston's hard fag porn, drip desire over Tom of Finland's impossibly muscled hyper-masculine drawings and try not to let lust stammer my tongue when I'm around the other butch girls. There is no room here for a sissy butch, and I don't want them to realize that I want to look like a boy but be treated like a skirt, that I shelter romantic dreams of pressing my cheek into a leather-covered back as we whiz away from the dyke bar on a motorcycle.

This summer I am in Las Vegas with a group of friends, all women. They decide to go to a shooting range, outvoting my budding-young-fag idea of a trip to the Liberace Museum. They fill up all the alleys in one range, so I go alone into the next one with my gun and my ammo.

Soon, a trio of men with rented handguns come in and attach paper targets to the clip before sending them whirring to the back of the range. They have selected the "hostage practice model" target, an unequalled classic for the red-blooded, heterosexual American male. It features a badly drawn, blonde, white lady in mid-1980's office attire, her mouth open in a helpless, pink-lipsticked "O". Holding her in one surly arm is a swarthy man of indeterminate Middle Eastern descent, wearing a green army jacket. He's holding a gun to her mouth in a way that artfully suggests a blowjob. The guys begin making loud, limping jokes—"Boy, I wish I could do this to the old lady during that time of the month!" as they empty their guns into her. I know they've noticed me, and I wonder what in the hell they're thinking, saying things like that in front of an obvious dyke with a loaded .38 Special and two full boxes of ammunition. Then I realize that, to them, I am just another one of the boys.

I am twenty-six, and I'm terrified that I *am* one of the boys. I've spent years in women's studies classes fretting that I subconsciously want to be a boy only because the future looks so comparatively dim as a girl. Through exciting, illicit, and sometimes dreaded study, I have obtained a "Tranny PhD" in The Art and Science of Breast Binding.

After extensive personal experimentation, I have isolated the three dominant methods. The first involves two too-small sports bras worn one on top of the other. This method leaves me feeling vaguely insulted, doubly un-athletic and more than a little like a sausage that has escaped its casing. The second is a complicated mummification of the upper body with several lengths of Ace bandage, whimsically accented with a topping of duct tape. Like all other tube tops, this concoction rolls up and down like a deranged window shade.

My clandestine favorite method involves a pair of control-top pantyhose, which I make my girly-girl girlfriend buy by the half-dozen at the grocery store. I cut the legs off at a slant and carefully cut out the crotch panel. Then I put my head through the crotch, my arms though the leg holes, and force the rest down over my chest. The end result is that my breasts look like they're about to rob a bank. Every one of these faux finishing efforts made for a prolonged, very ungainly striptease—and thus I credit them with my long dry spell of only giving, never receiving, sexual touch, always with my own clothes firmly on.

I am twenty-eight, and, like the Tony Bennett song, I have just left a part of my body in San Francisco. I took out a loan and, following a similar path as many people dissatisfied with their appearance, sought redemption in the dryly humorous ministrations of the best plastic surgeon my money could buy. As I am being prepped for my double mastectomy, the first surgery of my life, the nurse hands me a gown and paper booties, eyes me and says, "You look like someone who can get out of their clothes in two minutes, so I'll just come right back." I am still feeling conspicuously slutty as I am wheeled down the hall on my back.

For the first time in eleven years, I have a boyfriend. Apparently I'm more attracted to being any kind of queer than I am to women in particular. We share the same history of girlhood, and I am often surprised by the post-female freedom we have to be girlish with each other. I am his prom queen and, on select Sunday mornings, he channels Patsy Cline.

This is the year I earn my faggot merit badge by providing charitable oral relief to internet tricks, sad for and envious of the ability of men to separate the act of sex from whom they're performing it with. I have a few rude transsexual awakenings, like when I'm mirroring the guys jacking off in a porno and realize that far from playing the Big Organ, I'm fingering the World's Smallest Violin. My old girlfriend Melissa writes me a letter, describing the rage she feels at my transition, at my changing a body she so loved, saying she now feels like she let a man in her bed all those years ago.

I make a new friend—an elderly, devout, bi-weekly church-attending black woman who never bats an eye at my history. One afternoon, she will approach me after her doctor's appointment with a telling fear in her eyes and the question "What is a mastectomy like?" I will try to steady her for her unknown, and she will remind me how much I have suffered without the confidence of women.

Tonight I am thirty-three, and I am feeling conspicuously like a tomcat at the kitty club, fear gnawing through my every word that I am now an unwelcome stranger. I no longer belong in the community that I considered for a decade to be my only real refuge on earth. There are days when I regret writing myself out of it. I miss being a dyke. Its daily fears and challenges aside, I miss being visibly queer. Through the unwelcome force of habit, I still think of myself as a dyke sometimes, and I catch myself giving the "Hey, I see you and I'm one, too" nod to butches on the street. They read my greeting with confusion, or as sexual aggression, and return it with a glare or a protective arm around their girlfriend's shoulders. I work hard to remember—from where I am standing now—the comfort, the easy grin, the fearless sexiness of all-women's space. And I realize that despite my desire to flash my credentials at the door, I would bring something different to it now.

I will run out of legs far before I run out of communities in which I want to stand all at one time—my past as a dyke, my present as a guy, my reality as an FTM, my desire as a queer and my incredibly fractured self which feels indescribably lonely and, occasionally, unfathomably whole. In the dark, I'm a love story. I am Tony and Maria in "West Side Story," and I'm singing both parts of "A Place for Us." I am humming a tune with my mouth closed. I am hunkered down with my queer friends. I am biding my time. Frying my bacon. Playing my violin. And waiting for the door to crack, for a hand tipped with short fingernails to invite me in.

Age 29   Age 34

Magdelyn lives in the San Francisco Bay Area and works as a writer. Her writing has appeared in several magazines. She is also a recent graduate of Scarlot Harlot's Whore College.

Risky Business

"I am fond of children - except boys."
~**Lewis Carroll**

It was not yet dark, but everything was dim and fading away. The sun splashed on the horizon, drenching the clouds, as it began to sink. The sky dimmed. The sound of the surf crashing onto the Santa Monica Beach echoed against the laughter of us three unsupervised children running and playing on the sand; Joanna (my sister), Danielle and me. The sand felt cool under my bare feet, and squished between my toes. I was a strawberry-blonde, fair skinned, wisp of a child. Delicate. That's how people described me—so my mother tells me, "You were beautiful and people would ask, 'What's your daughter's name?'"

Out of the dusky, marine haze three young men crept into our lives. Their imitation Led Zeppelin-style long hair, and cannabis scent, failed to hide their predator instincts. The expansive beach was eerily abandoned. Alone, we were confronted by their unprovoked aggression. "Look at the three little girls," the short one said, peering at me. "You girls like to play naked?" His eyes stayed fixed on me. "Why don't you take your clothes off?"

It was obvious that I was not a girl. I was not wearing a dress or wearing barrettes in my hair. Hello Kitty was nowhere on my person. The young man's statement about "little girls" was not directed at my female companions. It was directed squarely at me. As a child, I could not understand that he was accusing me of a crime. The crime was that I was too feminine. Or, maybe, just not masculine enough. My violation was unintentional, but the implications were no less dangerous. He meant to attack my masculinity. But the real trespass was being forced to realize, from that moment on, that I could never again be just one of the girls.

We stood in terrified silence. The darkening sky blackened the water. The ocean looked lonely and ominous as it roared at us, like it was an inexplicable void to be feared—paradise lost.

Fade to black. (Pause)

Want me to tell you a story? Like happy endings? Fuck off. You won't find it here. Hollywood endings cost $10.50. Popcorn is extra. Rather, let me introduce myself. Meet Magdelyn, girl noir; a self-hating, self-destructive, profoundly lonely, stupid broad. I am the one in black, over by the bar. The one dressed like a whore, whispering to the bartender, "I'll have an apple martini."

Saturday night in the city. The bridge and tunnel frat/east-bay/mildly upper-middle class white kids are drinking the night away, with all the charm of slumming suburbanites. All the pretty, pretty people. I hate them. I prefer to be alone. I am uninterested in human interaction. I am empty inside. My soul slipped out. Maybe it's the antidepressants.

Martuni's is packed. A piano bar on the corner of Market and Valencia in San Francisco, it hosts a comfortable crowd. I'm the only transgendered person in the place. Within our culture of baggy, formless, earth-toned clothing that aspires to uninspired androgyny (ironically), I am dressed provocatively, with a Jacky O tinted ensemble, had Jackie O been a prostitute (no comment). The vanilla people give me side glances, as if they aren't looking. They are afraid to acknowledge whatever sin they think I am committing.

I finish my martini and reflect on the journey that led me to becoming Maggie. Who is Magdelyn? I am. I have always been her, and she has always been me. But in the beginning, she didn't have a name. There was no Magdelyn. There was just me—a distorted reflection in the mirror, an unwelcome image in photographs.

Had God been merciful and blessed me with two "X" chromosomes, I would have made a wonderful woman. I would've done him proud. Unfortunately, God misplaced one of my "X" chromosomes and I have struggled all my life trying to grasp some sense of self. It was like I could not breathe. Life itself was elusive, as if just out of my grasp. Deep within my core I knew, and know, that I am female. I have known it since I was a child.

"Children need love, especially when they do not deserve it."
~Harold Hulbert

My childhood was weird and isolated. I grew up in a Los Angeles neighborhood called Mt. Washington. Mt. Washington is hidden in plain view atop a hill, fifteen minutes from downtown. When I was growing up, it was home to ex-hippies, homosexuals in hiding, and a variety of eclectic people. Local eccentrics, like "Harpo Marx," populated the place. Harpo walked his dogs around the hill wearing go-go boots, inappropriately tight shorts with huge, garish belt buckles, and a head full of curly golden locks (like Harpo Marx). My neighbor, Vince, was a middle-aged letch—or is it more appropriate to say he was "sex-positive?" The neighborhood kids loved him. He drove around in a bright yellow 1932 Ford Deuce Coupe, grew pot in his back yard, and had a huge collection of porn. He held a yearly fencing tournament at a street party he hosted called the "Wazoo," featuring topless strippers serving drinks.

The weirdness could also hit closer to home. My friend, Gint, suffered through chaos when his mother became a punk rocker during her mid-life crisis. She wore dog collars and sported bruises and black eyes from slam dancing at places like the Los Angeles Palladium.

As interesting as it was, Mt. Washington was a lonely place to grow up. There was practically nothing within walking distance, and bicycles were impractical. The homes with kids were separated by long walks, canyons and steep hills. I would spend my days playing with dolls and pretending to be Wonder Woman, until I was too old for it to be considered cute. The isolation bred a community of bright, artistic, strange kids who were out of place almost everywhere they went.

My own sense of isolation grew as I got older and especially while I went through puberty. I suffered from a hormone imbalance, giving me a feminine butt, soft milky white skin, and a layer of female-like fat over my body. I'd gone from a skinny child, to a thin, but fleshy adolescent. My physical isolation mutated into psychological isolation. I didn't have the courage to present myself, within my community, in accordance with my identity. Conformity was much easier, violating community standards too dangerous. My experimentation had to take place in private or, if publicly, away from home.

I had no one to turn to. I was alone, unable to reach out for fear of rejection and ridicule within my surreal world. With no one on my side, there was no one to constructively criticize my attempts at self-feminization. There was no one to objectively tell me what was possible, and what was impossible. "Waiter! Reality check please."

In my early attempts at transformation, I did not realize the extent to which masculinization affected my appearance, nor how physically different I was from women. The subtle differences between the sexes are profound. We subconsciously identify and analyze scores of little sex markers, giving us the information we rely on to make determinations about who is a man, and who is a woman. As obvious as it may sound, women are not little men in dresses. In a sense, it is the opposite. Men are deformed women. Once the process of masculinization has occurred, hiding one's maleness beneath a layer of foundation is impossible.

My first attempts to present myself publicly as a woman were awkward. I did not know how to apply lipstick or coordinate an outfit. Since no one was around to help me, I had to self-assess my presentation. When I was old enough to drive, I left behind the strangling familiarity of Mt. Washington and escaped into the mysteries of the Los Angeles sprawl. I searched out tolerant venues for my gender expression, like

West Hollywood. I experimented with public expressions of the feminine, and exposed myself to the silent public criticism for the mirror image effect—I examined peoples' reactions to my presentation. Unfortunately, by the time I was capable of getting away from home, I had missed out on years of social education about the subtleties of *en femme* presentation. I'd wear ill-fitted clothing "borrowed" from my sister or mother. I'd wear panty hose, despite the discomfort, believing them a prerequisite for womanhood. My application of makeup was disastrous. But, my biggest problem was shoes. You know the situation is bad when you go out in public wearing a form-fitting skirt, an ill-fitting blouse, an emasculatingly tight pair of pantyhose, and wingtip shoes.

Each new attempt to present myself as a woman was more sophisticated than the prior attempt. Yet, each attempt was increasingly disheartening. The disappointments were profound, helping to nurture the first signs of a depression that would later come to cripple me.

Suicide Girl

The streets were wet from rain. I drove down Santa Monica Boulevard heading toward West Hollywood. Drizzle. My tires "swished" through the wet streets. The streetlights reflected off the glistening ground. I was upset, lonely, angry. I tried to hate God. But mostly, I hated myself.

I had not been out of the house for days. For the better part of a week, I laid down sleeping or inactively awake, staring at the walls, trying to find a reason to get out of bed. The room was filthy, the blankets smelled, I hadn't bathed in days. I ached from the inactivity, my muscles hurt, my head hurt and my spirits withered. When I finally managed to lift myself out of bed, I cleaned myself up and I left my apartment, trying to escape the isolation.

My form-fitting sheath dress was uncomfortably tight in the shoulders, but flattering to my curves. On my face was delicately applied white make-up, my lips washed with a mild pink lipstick, outlined in black. I penciled in wickedly arched eyebrows. The whole effect was that of a Gothic, jazz-age flapper, something F. Scott Fitzgerald and Mary Shelley would have conjured up, had they collaborated.

I slowed for a stop light. A young hitchhiker stood at the corner of the intersection. He tried to catch my eye—hopefully—through the intemperate weather. He was young, looked gay, and appeared desperate for a ride. I begrudgingly pulled over. He sprinted to the passenger side door. He smelled of clove cigarettes, a kind of pleasant, sweet cinnamony fragrance. "You look amazing," he says. I take this as a throwaway compliment. Meaningless. "What are you doing tonight?" he asks. He wants a ride to Circus of Books. I have no destination. I will find myself somewhere, with someone. I always do. I make "friends" easily. "Why don't you come in with me," he says, "I'm meeting somebody." If I go with him, he will pressure me for sex, not because I am a woman, but because he thinks I am gay. I drop him off. He leans over, places his hand on the skin of my thigh, and kisses my cheek. "Bye." He slams the door, knocking the rain drops from the window. I am glad he's gone. I don't want to meet anyone. I just want to be happy by myself. I want to be happy with myself.

The rain gets heavy. I listen to it ricochet off the roof. I can't bring myself to waste another night self-sacrificing in some un-extraordinary dark room where the music is too loud, same people, different faces, sipping drinks and choking down cigarettes. I feel my search for happiness is futile. I drive home.

I start a warm bath and swish the water around, feeling it for temperature. I retrieve a sharp paring knife from the kitchen. In my room, I sit on the edge of my unmade bed, and I slit my wrist. Three deep, parallel cuts from my palm down, let my blood spill. I watch the blood trail down my arm. A few drops spill on my thigh and fall to my distressed leather, snip-toed shoes.

I stand up and look in the mirror. The mirror makes me look thinner than I really am. There I am—Magdelyn—dressed to impress. Suddenly, I realize I am killing the wrong person. It is not Magdelyn I want dead. It is the male me I want to destroy. I press my palm onto the wounds. I drop the knife and cry. The tears smudge my mascara. Charcoal grey streams run down my face. I call an ambulance.

Magdelyn Does San Francisco

I needed to get out. I was living two separate lives in Los Angeles. My self-induced schizophrenia meant that I was two people. The more that I became Magdelyn, the more Magdelyn competed for time, resources and attention. It came to the point where Magdelyn was not just part of me, but instead a totally separate person. Both of my identities had their own sets of friends, experiences, and aspirations. The male me tried to conform to expectations and maintain the stability of my family and friends. Magdelyn, on the other hand, was growing up without guidance. The lessons she learned were taught through ugly experiences by ugly people who manipulated and used her. Both aspects of me were self-destructive.

It was time to stop wasting time. I needed to begin the transition. Brief forays in and out of Magdelyn's world were not enough. I needed to commit to that which I already knew. I am Magdelyn. As luck would have it, I had the opportunity to move to San Francisco. It was an environment in which Magdelyn could grow. I experimented with my style and refined my look. My self-styled presentation was the physical manifestation of my inner feelings. I would eventually come to see myself both mentally and physically as Magdelyn.

Although I did not live full-time as a woman, the relationship between Magdelyn and my male-self reversed. Whereas Magdelyn had previously been only a guest in my life, it was now her male counterpart who intruded. I felt that I could not completely transition because the male part of me held all the credentials and work experience. It was like a marriage in which the wife has given up her life for her spouse, and has no work or credit history. Trying to change my gender and also negotiate the financial aspect of my life was too difficult for me to handle. I would wait to completely transition. I also decided not to present myself as a woman to my family while my father was still alive. He was a beautiful and charming man. But he would never accept me as his daughter.

I was inspired to start transitioning by a book entitled, *Kim* by Kim Harlow, with photographs by Bettina Rheins. Kim Harlow's unfinished autobiography details her life as a transsexual woman. She never finished the book because she died of AIDS. The photographs of Kim look out from the pages with a heart-wrenching blank expression that communicates desperation and the tragedy of a life cut short. The self-doubt she expresses in her words, the angst, and sorrows parallel my own.

If Kim Harlow's story was my inspiration to begin transitioning, the greatest impact to my self-image in the beginning came from my self-administration of hormones and testosterone blockers. Girl juice is easy to get. I just ordered it over the internet, no prescription necessary. Overseas distributors have web pages exclusively for transgendered people.

The psychological effect of the girl juice cocktail was as important as the physical changes that took place. Testosterone is a poison. It deforms your body and slants your perspective, distorting your thoughts. When I started taking estrogen and T-blockers, my mind cleared. I calmed down. I slowed down. My interest in sex stopped being a nuisance and my interest in trying to develop personal relationships grew.

The physical changes were also welcome. My breasts started to develop. The process was painful because of both the enlarging mammary glands, as well as the tender nipples. My curves, already feminine-like, became more pronounced, so that even in men's clothes my butt was noticeably large and my waist small, so that my trousers dropped down my waist and rested on my hips. With the psychological and physical changes, I felt ready to reach out and have a social life.

"One who looks for a friend without faults will have none."
~Hasidic Saying

"You're a train wreck," Molly tells me. She doesn't mean it in a nice way. Molly is a trans friend of mine. I don't have many trans friends, preferring to stay away from the campiness and drama of trans society. Molly and I usually talk via instant messaging. On this occasion we meet over drinks at the weekly transwomen get-together she organizes. I am sipping a Bloody Mary. I love Bloody Marys. They almost taste like food. I usually don't attend. I don't understand the other women. They look like men in dresses. Some of them don't even try to look like women. Most don't take hormones. Their attempts at feminization, both physically and socially, borders on the cartoonish. I always find it disconcerting when transwomen start talking football.

Molly and I talk about my "boyfriend," a.k.a. my internet stalker. He is a chef. Somehow he found me on the internet and began sending me e-mails. The e-mails started with him wanting to rescue me from my life and take care of me. They escalated to him demanding my phone number, and chastising me for not giving it to him. He would give me orders and then verbally discipline me for not following them. He seemed to think he had an ownership interest in me. Scores of instant messages would appear on my computer while I was away. It got to the point that I was afraid he would somehow track me down. The kicker was when he sent me a photograph of himself in his chef outfit, holding two knives. Molly says I bring these things on myself.

Molly says she likes me, but I feel she doesn't respect me. I know why. I am an erratic person, inconsistent, with a self-destructive streak. She is frustrated that I don't attend her gathering more often. She is appalled that I cut myself when I get depressed. She called me a drama queen when she saw the scars on my wrist.

She sits across the table with her easy charm, criticizing me with her elegant English accent for my careless adventure in the Tenderloin the night before. I'd gone to the Tenderloin with a few friends for drinks, dressed like a skank. I had gotten sauced and crept through the seediest parts of the neighborhood on my way home, among the drug dealers and trans-whores, through which I move effortlessly and feel quite comfortable.

You can meet some really interesting people at 2 a.m. in the Tenderloin. Like when I met a potential pimp. I was minding my own business, walking on Post Street toward Polk, when a young (real young) black girl asks me for a cigarette.

"Sorry," I say without feminizing my voice.

"You a guy?" she asks.

She follows me. "For real?" she says aggressively, "You better get me my money bitch! You gonna get me my money, bitch? You better get my money, bitch!" I ignore her. I continue walking. We approach a black guy all gangsta'd out leaning against the wall of a bodega. The girl gets even more aggressive as we approach him. "You better fuckin' get me my money, bitch!" I kind of enjoyed the objectification. Hell, I would have let her pimp me.

Anyway, back to why Molly is upset with me. I walk up Polk and am about to cross Hemlock when a shiny new silver Mercedes stops in front of me. A desperately nervous middle-eastern man, in his fifties, bald and heavy set (not fat) cracks his window. He says something I can't make out as the car doors unlock. He motions me to get it. I'm stunned for a moment. I bend over and ask timidly, "You wanna date?" As soon as I ask the question, I start panicking about how I am going to gracefully escape the situation.

"Yes," he mumbles, waving his hand furiously at me to get in. He looks frustrated, even a little angry that I haven't opened the door. Nervous, I start to walk around the car. Just as I step away, a police cruiser slows down near me. The man in the Mercedes drives down Hemlock. I pretend not to notice the black-and-white. I quickly join a line of people who are waiting for an I.D. check before entering Vertigo bar. I reach into my purse as if to pull out my I.D. As I rustle around my purse, I think to myself, "Wow! What a great improv." When the police continue up Polk, I continue to Sutter.

At the corner of Sutter and Polk, I am again greeted by the Mercedes driving guy. He stops again. "What are you doing? There are black-and-whites everywhere, and you're dragging your feet." I find his condescending tone flattering, like it indicates I am a real girl. I guess I'm just sick that way. "Where are you staying?" he asks. "I'm not staying anywhere," I reply. "I'm not from the city," he says. His demeanor lightens to familiarity, like we are good friends now. "How much?" he says, nervously. He has reason to be nervous. The place is crawling with cops. A grey Taurus aggressively pulls up right in front of him. "Cops," he states. I step away from the window. He pulls away.

A black-and-white turns the corner. I walk over and lean against a lamppost. The cops look me over, deciding whether or not to stop and harass me. They continue on, slowly. The passenger-side patrolman keeps a suspicious eye on me. Getting arrested could do me some good. Maybe it would kick me out of the malaise-induced fog that blurs my thoughts.

Molly disapproves of me. I am hurt. I like her. I want her to like me. She says she does. She would never end our friendship—if that is what it is—because with my striking presentation and sinful air, I am a magnet for society otherwise unavailable to her. But, just the same, she feels compelled to counsel me. She doesn't do it gently. She says I am unstable. She says my self-administration of hormones is dangerous, my behavior reckless. Molly says I need to go see a doctor. Maybe she is right.

Before I take you along to see my doctor, let me address a question that may be on your mind. From the last few paragraphs, you may be asking yourself, "Is Maggie a whore?" The question of transwomen and prostitution is a fetish for society. I don't believe there is anything wrong with having an interest in the subject, or being titillated by any particular form of consensual, adult sexuality. But, I will not answer the question, not because I want to protect my reputation (such as it is) nor because I am shy about my personal life. It's just too cliché and, on the whole, irrelevant to my life path. Okay. Okay. I will say this. I have never been arrested for prostitution.

Heal Thyself

Finding a doctor in San Francisco, with experience administering care to the transgendered community, is not as easy as you would think. After weeks of searching, I came across Dr. Charles Moser. I called his office for an appointment. His staff was cordial, but insistent. They required a letter from a therapist stating that I was suffering from Gender Identity Disorder before I could see the good doctor. "Oh, great," I thought to myself, "Another plan—a plan by the man to keep a sister down." Luckily, I had previously been in and out of therapy. I had a relationship with Patrick Califia, a therapist who works with the transgendered community. Patrick is a transman and author of a veritable library of books with titles like *Sex Changes: The Politics of Transgenderism* and *Speaking Sex to Power*.

I called Patrick, in desperation. As the phone rang, I was wary of rejection. Like all my relationships, I had neglected my relationship with Patrick through my erratic and inconsistent behavior. Burning bridges is a specialty of mine. (People incorrectly interpret my inconsistency as being disrespectful or dismissive.) I left a voice mail—beginning with, "I hope you remember me..."—and intoned the best conciliatory vibe I could conjure. I can be very pathetic when I need to be.

Patrick got in touch with me, stating that he'd be happy to write the letter. He would also like to see how my transition was coming along since the last time we got together. I scheduled a session with him. The session was late in the day. I got off work at five and had to fill a couple of hours before seeing him. I jumped on a streetcar on Market Street, just to take the ride and look at the passing people. When I reached the Castro, I detrained and walked around, window shopping. I decided to have a drink. Twin Peaks is the bar that sits at the acute corner angle of 17th and Market. It was born in the defiant era of gay activism that spearheaded San Francisco's "out" movement in the 1970's. I went in, and ordered an apple martini.

A woman at the bar reached out and touched the small of my back. "You look beautiful, honey." Her hand stayed right above my ass for a few uncomfortable moments. I smiled awkwardly. For some reason, women and gay men really like my look. I think it is the dramatic, retro sexuality that educated women now think inappropriately deferential to the patriarchy. I have been accused by other transpeople of being a sexist because of my interpretation of femininity. Maybe women like that I emphasize my curves, which harks back to an earlier perception of the feminine—out of style today—built on a 5'10" frame made taller with heels. "Thank you," I whisper. I dislike compliments. I hate to be made self-aware. I really don't like myself. I am insecure.

I take my apple martini, delicately navigating the stairs to the balcony overlooking the bar where I can be alone. My body tries to extract nutrients from the poison. I have been starving myself, trying to lose weight, and haven't eaten anything for almost two days. My anorexia is kicking in again. Unfortunately, for my body, there are no apples in my martini. I finish it and get another. As I sip the second one, the alcohol starts to hit me hard. I become emotional and cry. Tears stream down my face. I try to control myself. I have to leave to make my appointment, but I can't stop crying. I walk downstairs, weeping. I set the glass on the blurry bar. The queens all turn and look at me as I leave. Their faces express subtly concealed disgust, like, "What is this stupid bitch crying about?" I have experienced open hostility from some gay men, whom I think really dislike male-to-female trans folk.

I cry all the way to the appointment. I break down during the session in a humiliating demonstration of self-pity. I spill out the self-hatred and tell Patrick about the disconnect between my ability to easily charm people, and my total failure to keep long-term relationships. I try to give examples of my plight with allegory and analogy, but my attempts at illustration turn out to be just simple observations about myself that I had just never articulated before. I am alone because I don't know how not to be alone. My unhappiness is a selfish self-indulgence. I am not happy because I don't want to be happy. My life has been bifurcated between the male me, and Magdelyn. The two are not complimentary and each has sucked from the other vital skills for survival. Each has wrecked the other's life.

Needless to say, I have been in therapy ever since.

Patrick wrote the letter for me, but insisted on including that I needed to be checked out for depression. As I prepared for my appointment with Dr. Moser, I tried to formulate how I would communicate my state of mind. I didn't want to say that I am transgendered in a conclusive manner. Nor did I want to speak clichés like "I am a woman in a man's body," which has been relegated to punch line status. I wanted to make him understand me. I tried to prepare an excuse for myself. I wanted him to understand that it wasn't my fault.

As I wrote earlier, my inspiration for transition came largely from Kim Harlow. Her life experience was compelling. I hated her for her beauty. But, her tragedy was magnetic. Yet, she was just one of many inspirations. In one way or another, I want to be Aeon Flux and Amélie, Louise Brooks and Kim Harlow. I variously wanted to skip stones over the river Seine, and be a Monacan assassin. I want to look out in black and white from a noir picture screen with big, innocent eyes wrapped in a wickedly erotic aura; freak of nature cool broad, Goth chic, angular lines, and a body that assaults with "what the fuck are you looking at" sex. I want to speak in dramatic riddles, and die because of my own incompetence. If none of this makes sense to you, that is all right. It doesn't make sense to me either. These are just the dreams I have, fleeting sensations—an inadequate expression of feelings from deep within me. Somehow, I had to communicate all that to Dr. Moser.

But I could not think of an explanation for my existence, or an excuse for my feelings. As I sat in the examination room, waiting for Dr. Moser, I felt queasy and unprepared. Dr. Moser entered and I looked him over. He was short, clean but seemed disheveled, with salt and pepper curly hair, and a manicured beard. He wore a Star Trek badge on his lab coat.

"You are a Trekky?" I asked.

"You saw that, huh?" he replied.

"I like the old ones. I used to watch them with my father."

"I like them all," he said.

He had me take off my clothes. He sat down, and spoke to me matter-of-factly, taking a long detailed medical and family history. He did not moderate his speech with the superficial friendly intonation that I am used to when I am Magdelyn. He took the most thorough physical I have ever had. The irony of being a transgendered woman is having both a prostate exam and a breast exam during the same physical examination.

After all was said and done, he prescribed me Lexapro (an anti-depressant), a T-blocker and estrogen in a smaller dose than I was taking while self-medicating. He prescribed blood tests and told me I had been overdosing on hormones. He wanted me to use estrogen patches instead of pills because there was less danger of blood clots. I left his office with a giddy sense of my own identity.

I had trouble filling the prescriptions. I had to explain why my prescription said "Magdelyn," but my driver's license said something else. It was a strange conversation to have while people waited behind me to pick up their pills. The lowered doses prescribed by Dr. Moser resulted in my body reacting like I was going through menopause. I had night sweats and hot flashes. I had trouble sleeping through the night. The symptoms eventually went away, and the psychological effects have diminished; my self-hatred has been mitigated and my self-image improved.

I now feel I have people on my side. I have a doctor who understands me. I have a therapist who is familiar with my issues. I have started to make friends both in and out of the trans community. In essence, I have started to live my life. I have been alive ever since. Occasionally, I even feel happy. So there. That is your Hollywood ending. Cough up the $10.50.

Age 31

Lee Maranto is originally from southern California but has called northern California home since his college days. Lee currently works in higher education with an intention to complete his law degree within the next five years. He enjoys spending time with his partner and friends, playing poker and educating on social justice issues.

Reflections on Being a Real Man

A few years ago, I was at a party. I went as a favor to my best friend. He had a new lady in his life and I was enlisted to be his "wing man." He needed some company because he knew no one at this party and he didn't want to arrive solo. I went, although I was not feeling my usual social self. As I expected, he became quite enamored with his new companion and I was left to fend for myself. I successfully dodged the attempted force-feeding of pot truffles and heavy flirtation of the host, a lovely, yet extremely intoxicated gay man. Having smoked a lot of cigarettes already, I decided to have one more, nurse my last drink and head out. While sitting outside and trying to be invisible, a beautiful long-haired, brunette woman asked me for a light. I complied and she sat down. We started to chat and began a nice conversation. She was from Australia, so I was immediately enchanted by her accent. It turned out that she knew no one at the party either. She was a new neighbor in the building and was invited by our friendly host. Having bonded over our mutual discomfort, we continued our chat and ensuing flirtation. The wine continued to flow (thanks to our attentive host) and we carried on for another hour or so.

I could tell that she was attracted to me. And perhaps due to the wine, or my gentlemanly charm, we began to move closer together. She was about 15 years my senior, but was impressed with the maturity of my 26 years. We talked about our jobs, our passions, our friends and our love of travel. I mentioned having a single mom and how I still sent her flowers every year for her birthday. I could tell that this struck a particularly romantic chord with her. We moved closer together. I took a risk and placed my hand on her thigh. She indicated to me (the way that women do) that it was a welcomed touch. Emboldened by the alcohol in my system and encouraged by her smile, I leaned forward and kissed her. This act was also well received. Neither of us concerned by any potential onlookers, we quite passionately began making out. We continued like this for quite a while. As we edged closer to transgressing the line of acceptable PDA (public displays of affection), I decided we should seek a more private venue. I asked her where her place was. She stood up and had me follow her down to her apartment.

The party was in the attic apartment of the building and she lived on the ground floor. As we said our goodbyes to others and headed down the stairs, I observed that she was very intoxicated. She slipped down the stairs a little and I became concerned that I was getting myself into a situation from which it would be difficult to extricate myself. As much as I wanted to have sex with this woman, I would not be able to and I began to strategize how I could back out of my implied intention to do so. I couldn't help but think that if circumstances were different, I would be able to have this one night stand that was clearly desired by both parties. I fantasized about how great the encounter would be for the both of us. We could have a nice evening together and I would wake up, put on my clothes from the night before and head home. I already knew, there was no way that was going to happen…

We got downstairs and ended up at her door. We kissed some more. I tried to maintain my prior state of engagement, but I was now preoccupied with planning my escape. Then, she opened the door and we stumbled into her apartment. She walked me to her bed and we began kissing and making out some more. She pushed me back onto the bed and climbed on top of me.

Now, in a parallel universe where I'm a regular guy, this is a fantasy come to life. I have a sexy woman who has made it very clear to me that she would like to fuck me and be fucked by me. The idea of such a scenario was very enticing and I got sucked into this fantasy and went with it. Yes, I think to myself. I'm with her. Let's do this.

I'm almost ready to abandon my escape plan…

Then she starts fumbling with my shirt. She doesn't know that I have three layers of shirts on. She manages to get past the first one without too much resistance. Next, she goes for the second one. This is a more difficult task as it is tucked into my pants. Finally, successfully liberating the second shirt, she encounters the third shirt. This discovery evokes a sigh of frustration and a small, sexy grunt. Meanwhile, I'm trying to think fast about how to rewind the last 45 minutes. As I fail to come up with a viable plan in the 30 seconds I have, she has since started to unbuckle my belt and I know that my pants will be next. At this point, instinct kicks in and I decide to distract her.

In a forceful, yet sexy maneuver, I flip her over and proceed to unbutton *her* pants. I get her jeans undone to discover that she is not wearing any underwear.

My parallel universe self has a moment of despair as I think about how differently this evening could have gone in that world.

Now that her jeans are off, I kiss her some more. While I'm kissing her, I undo her blouse and unclasp her bra. She is now completely naked. I am not. I have managed in this process to only remove my shoes and keep all other clothing firmly attached to my body, sans one shirt.

While still kissing her, I go on autopilot and start navigating her body with my hands. I start at her head with kisses on her lips and neck. With this, she starts to go for my pants again. So I take her hands, lift them over her head and lay her down. I move my head down to her breasts where I spend some time. My new plan is to go down on her. I figure that if I make her orgasm, she might fall asleep and I can slip out. It won't be so bad, because she'll have gotten something out of this encounter and hopefully won't feel used.

I haven't really thought this plan through very much, but it's all I've got at this point.

I focus on keeping her aroused and going down on her. I'm successful at completing my task at hand. Afterward, she pulls me up to her and we kiss some more. I'm gearing up to have a short cuddle and say my goodbyes. Meanwhile, she goes for my pants again. I couldn't help but think to myself that I never thought I would have to fend off a woman like this (nor did I ever think to myself that I would ever want to).

To break her momentum, I decided that I needed to go to the bathroom. I used the time to gather myself and come up with a new plan. I decided to tell her that I had to leave, as my friends would be wondering what happened to me. I secretly hoped that she was too drunk to remember that I already mentioned that I was free with absolutely no obligation in the morning.

When I returned from the bathroom, she greeted me with some more kisses. I sat down on the bed with her so I could break the news. I told her that I had to leave. She replied with a shocked and disappointed tone, "Noooo." I added that I had breakfast plans in the morning with my friends and had to meet them early. As I explained this to her, I reached for my shoes and began putting them on my feet. She watched me with a confused and almost devastated look. It was very clear to me that she didn't understand what was happening at all.

I wondered what she thought might be going on. I mean, what could possibly make a young guy pass up an opportunity like this with a sexy and more-than-willing, erotically-charged woman? I ran through the possibilities in my mind, in preparation for having to provide an excuse. I was fully prepared to tell her that I was too drunk to get hard and leave it at that. I was perfectly willing to accept being "that guy" in order to be able to get out of this situation. However, given her enthusiasm, I was afraid that she would try to alleviate my "condition." So, I opted to not mention anything about my "condition" and insist on leaving.

As I tied my shoelaces, I firmed up my game plan and decided to stick with what I told her. I got up to kiss her one last time to say goodbye. And partly out of guilt for leaving her like this and partly out of a desire to affirm to her that I was indeed a good lover, but would never really get to show her, I went down on her again. After she came, I kissed her again for the last time and left.

As I walked down the hallway of the apartment building, I couldn't help but remember a scene out of *Stone Butch Blues*, a book by Leslie Feinberg that I read early into my transition and was pretty influential for me. Jess, the protagonist has a similar encounter with a woman who doesn't know about his history. In the book, the two have sex. When I read that scene, I was intrigued about Jess's ability to have intercourse without having to negotiate the difficult conversation about his body. For a fleeting moment, I was envious at the thought of "pulling it off." Then I was struck with a feeling of shame and remorse, no doubt imputed from what would have happened had I not walked away. I was not interested in having that feeling of emptiness and isolation for myself. And as I hopped into my truck, sobered by the experience, I was glad that I left when I did. I was sorry to have to leave the way that I did, but the alternative would not have been acceptable. I was again reminded of the isolation, fear, discontent, frustration, anger and betrayal of my body and who I was in this world. In a way that I had never felt it before, I felt the anguish of what it means to be transgender. On this evening, I was reminded of the complexity and negotiation of interpersonal relations that I would continue to face the rest of my life as a result of my choice to live my life as a man.

At the time that I made that decision, I was 21 and I really had no idea what it really meant to live as man in our society. I just knew that it wasn't going to work out to continue to live as something in between a man and woman anymore. I had been raised an only child, by a single mom. I grew up visiting my mom's three sisters and their husbands. My interactions with my uncles always felt awkward. I felt kinship and connection with my aunts, but I identified more with my uncles.

Once I decided to go forward with my physical transition, I was not prepared for how my life experience might change. I was aware that I would feel different in the world, but I was not fully aware of how the world would change in its relation to me. Specifically, this shift would be most present in the privileges I would now get as a white man. These privileges would become ever so clear to me early on in my transition. On the morning of my court date for my official name change (an important day for any transperson), I experienced a life-changing moment.

My girlfriend, K, and I had arrived a little early. We were not scheduled to be in a courtroom, but a bungalow where it seemed like the overflow cases were sent. At the time, K and I were the only folks there. This was about two months before I started testosterone, so it was a toss-up whether I was passing as male or not. In fact, I assumed most of the time that I was not passing as male. After we were there for a few minutes, a woman walked up and waited for the door to be opened, as we were doing. I remember very clearly that she was wearing a grey skirt suit ensemble with a white blouse. She was blonde with her hair up and she carried a briefcase. I would guess that she was in her late twenties. I remember it so clearly because I thought she was very attractive, so attractive that I checked her out pretty intently. *I always did have a thing for women in power suits.* I scanned her up and down, noting that she had nice legs. Soon thereafter, K hit me on the arm and exclaimed, "I can't believe you just did that!"

"What?!?" I retorted. Completely lost in my own thoughts, I was unaware of myself and my actions.

"We'll talk later about this." She responded angrily. This was an unusual tone for her.

I still didn't know what she was talking about. When I looked back at the woman, I noticed her body language had shifted. She seemed scared or vulnerable. Her knees were turned inward and she wasn't making eye contact with me. Worried that she had heard the exchange between me and K, and more importantly, heard my very unmasculine voice, I assumed that she was uncomfortable with her perception of me as a butch dyke. This angered me. Not only was I angry that I was invisible as the man that I felt myself to be, but I felt like she was being homophobic. Feeling that fear, I began to posture myself in an aggressive way. I was not going to be made to feel ashamed of myself by this woman in her skirt power suit.

Her response was to retreat further into her body. In fact, if we weren't standing together outside this bungalow, I would have said that her body language was consistent with someone who was naked in front of a stranger. This didn't make a whole lot of sense to me, as it didn't seem fitting to the situation, as I understood it to be. But nevertheless, I felt that I was able to own the space and thus not feel marginalized because of my queer identity.

The bungalow/courtroom was then opened. I never looked at the woman again. I became pretty involved in my court proceeding. I was nervous that the judge was going to call me by my given name in front of all these people, so I was busy mentally preparing for this occurrence. When my file came up on the docket, I was pleasantly surprised to hear the judge refer to me by my chosen name and not my given name. Elated and grateful with being spared the humiliation I had anticipated, I walked out feeling victorious and happy. This was a major milestone for me in my transition.

As soon as we got in the car, K reminded me of the scene outside the bungalow. I listened to her as she explained how I unabashedly looked that woman up and down. And given how attractive she was, we could assume that this was part of her daily experience. Confused about what I thought the interaction was about, I shared that I thought that she was being homophobic, because I was not passing a lot at that time. She reminded me that we were outside of our queer confines in this courtroom setting. And given that the courtroom was the most mainstream environment we had encountered in our little liberal town, I realized that I was presenting male and likely being perceived as such. Then I remembered that the judge never used my old name, so as far as this woman was concerned, I was a guy.

I was horrified. If I was really passing, that means I must have looked like I was 17 or 18 years old. Could a 17-year-old boy really make an older, professional woman feel like that? I couldn't quite believe that that was the power dynamic. *It was so easy to take from her.* The image of her retreating into herself was burned in my mind and I was disgusted with myself.

At the time, I was a college student and a member of a social justice organization. We did educational workshops on oppression and intersections of power and privilege. I identified as a feminist and was proud to do so given that I was in the middle of transitioning into a man. I was proud that I would be carrying that value system into my new life and was eager to continue my work around sexism. I couldn't believe that I had just done what had been described to me. It was awful. I was embarrassed and ashamed. I was also hurt. I was hurt to know that I had done something so awful to this woman and I would never see her again. I would never get to apologize or let her know that I wasn't really like that. In her mind now, I was like every other man she had experienced in her life. But I knew I was different. I was going to be the guy educating other men on how to not do this very thing. It was sad to me that she would never know any of that.

When I think of this story now, I still feel the sadness that I contributed to a form of violence in this woman's life and I'm not ever going to be able to make amends for it. However, I'm also grateful. I'm grateful to K for being strong enough to point it out to me. This hard lesson was not lost on me. In fact, I remember it often, along with all my feelings about it, so that I never do it again. I'm grateful because this was an important moment in my life as a man. I would hazard to guess that not many men will ever experience such a lesson on the responsibility and power they wield as men in our society.

It is that power and responsibility that I take very seriously now. Since then, I have been living full-time as male. I have had many opportunities to think critically about the position that I occupy in the world. I went from a poor, white, dyke, to an educated, white, straight man. When I take my girlfriend's hand while walking down the street, I'm reminded that I couldn't always do that. When I get pulled over by a police officer, I'm reminded that I'm given the benefit of the doubt when they let me off with a warning. When I suggest an idea in a staff meeting at work, I'm reminded that others think it's a valuable contribution because it's taken seriously. This is my daily experience now. And I keep myself engaged with these things by having these conversations with myself and other white men.

Negotiating my maleness has been a journey. Early on in my transition, I felt very insecure around my masculinity. I thought it was because I was trans, but as I grow older in this male world, I've learned that my insecurity was based more on society's poorly defined notion of maleness. Becoming a man the way that I did allowed me to take a lot of ownership over what kind of man I wanted to be. It has been my observation that a lot of men who were born male haven't had that experience with their maleness. That observation has allowed me to have more compassion for men and young boys than I used to. Having been through the physical and mental process of becoming male, I've learned that being a "man" doesn't have to be about being an "alpha dog" or the guy taking up the most space in the room. I've been able to take comfort in the fact that a real "man" is one who has integrity, honors women, is accountable for his actions, listens and is tender. Ultimately, a real "man" takes responsibility for how our society responds to his presence in this world. It is by this standard that I would like to be measured when my time in this life comes to an end.

Age 43   Age 51

Shannon Weckman is a 56-year-old woman living in Felton, California. She is currently retired following a long and varied career in the computer field. Her hobbies include hiking in the redwoods, gardening, photography, and model railroading.

The Details of Becoming a Woman

"Jimmy, open that door right now!" my mother yelled. I was pulling the skirt off as fast as I could, stuffing it into a brown paper bag and looking for a place to hide it. The best place seemed to be on the floor behind the toilet, even though it showed. "Open that door right now!" she yelled again. I was getting dressed really fast. Then, scared to death, heart pounding rapidly, I opened the door, walked into the hallway and headed toward a bedroom where my brothers were playing. My mother glanced my way but didn't say anything. I started playing with my brothers, worried whether my mother would find the bag I had hidden and wondering how I was going to get it out of the bathroom and safely put away.

It wasn't long before my mother wandered into the bathroom and found the bag; she opened it and pulled out a black skirt, which I had previously cut shorter in length. She had a puzzled look on her face. She headed for the bedroom where I was playing with my brothers and, holding the skirt out toward me, asked if it was mine. I answered "no" trying to look innocent. She had me and my brothers line up and she asked each one of us, "Who does this belong to?" holding out the empty brown bag and black skirt. Each of us answered, "It's not mine." After several attempts to determine who the owner was, she gave up and left the room.

I guess I shouldn't be surprised that my mother was pounding on the door wanting me out of the bathroom. After all, this wasn't the first time I had gone in there and stayed for a long time. As young as I was, it probably never occurred to me just how long I was tying up the bathroom or that anyone would notice. It was the one place I knew I could have privacy by locking the door. Then I could cross-dress without fear. At least that's what I thought at the time.

Cross-dressing is something I have done for as long as I can remember. Certainly I was cross-dressing when I was in the third grade. I had a girlfriend, too, so I remember those times well. I was discovering myself sexually and had begun masturbating. Cross-dressing was erotic and sexually exciting for me and continued to be for many years.

By the way, my name was James. I was born in Louisville, Kentucky. During my childhood, I remember looking up to female figures such as my mother, my aunt, my grandmother, and wishing that I could be more like them. During recess at school, I would always look over at the girls playing and wish that I could be with them instead of with the boys. Boys tended to play rough and be more competitive; something that just didn't feel right for me.

As I got older, there were times when I was left alone at home and these were special times for me. They afforded me the opportunity to experiment with dressing like a girl, wearing different clothing such as slips, skirts, dresses, panties, bras and high heels. It was sort of an obsession and I could get totally immersed in it, but always had to be ready to quickly change into my boy clothes should someone come home unexpectedly.

My bedroom was located in the front of the house. There I could cross-dress keeping one eye on the driveway through the Venetian blinds that covered the window and I could also hear should a car pull in. Our home had a basement and I would frequently go down there when the rest of the family was watching TV and secretly and cautiously experience cross-dressing. It was certainly more exciting to me than what might have been on TV that evening.

The family was growing. I had three brothers and my mother was expecting. My parents had decided it was time to move into a larger home and, as part of that plan, we temporarily moved into my grandmother's home. This is where my only sister was born and died about 30 days later of SIDS.

My parents then purchased a larger home a couple of miles from my grandmother's house. I had initially moved in with the rest of the family but then had a disagreement with my mother, walked out, and ended up staying with my grandmother. To my surprise, my mother brought my clothes over and allowed me to continue to stay there. I was a big help to my grandmother and it was close to school, so it turned out to be advantageous for my mother to let me stay.

Staying with my grandmother provided me with lots of time to myself. I had more time to study, which resulted in better grades, and plenty of time to cross-dress since I had my own room and access to the attic from my bedroom. I would frequently go up into the attic and cross-dress after my grandmother went to bed.

One day, I was dressed as a girl, roaming around my grandmother's backyard, when I heard a car pull into the driveway. Out of the corner of my eye, I saw my mother get out of the car and head for the front porch. What was I to do? I was standing there in a blouse and skirt outside the house. I couldn't go in and I couldn't just leave. I heard my mother calling, "Jimmy! Jimmy!" She was looking for me. I ducked under the back porch. I was bent over and crouched way down when I heard my mother's footsteps as they came out onto the porch. "Jimmy," she called. She opened the porch door and began to come down the steps into the backyard. What could I do? I was helpless. What was going to happen? Would she see me under the porch? She walked into the backyard away from the house looking for me, then turned around facing the back of the house and saw me there under the porch. I could have died. She asked, "What are you doing under there?" On all fours, I crawled out from under the porch, scurried up the porch steps and headed straight for the bathroom where I changed into my male clothes. I was so embarrassed!

After getting back into my male clothes, I came out of the bathroom and she was waiting for me in the living room, motioning for me to sit down. She asked, "Why were you wearing girl's clothes?" I quickly responded, "I just wanted to see how it felt." She appeared to accept my answer and we never spoke of it again. After that, I was more careful about my cross-dressing, but it continued.

Following high school, I worked summers and went to college for two years. This was followed by my decision to join the Air Force. The Vietnam War was going on and a lottery drawing was held to determine who got drafted first. I was going to get drafted by the Army for certain since I had a low lottery number. In my opinion, joining the Air Force was a better decision. And I didn't have to go to Vietnam.

At twenty years of age, right after basic training, I entered my first marriage to a young lady I met in high school. My marriage was normal enough and I secretly continued my cross-dressing. The best opportunities for cross-dressing were when she attended church or went shopping. In both cases, she was usually gone for hours. I never even considered telling her about it. It was something I did not want to share and I like to believe that she would have simply thought that it was dumb. After about five years, we seemed to be headed in different directions so we got a divorce.

I received an "early out" of the Air Force with an honorable discharge to return to college. I attended Central State University, Edmond, Oklahoma. I graduated with a B.S. in Computer Science in 1977 and then with an MBA, a year later. Following college, I worked for companies in Tulsa, Oklahoma and Dallas, Texas.

Hair. I hated being a hairy male. In fact, I started using hair clippers to trim arm and leg hair to a shorter, less noticeable, length. I tried different things to get rid of the hair on my face, such as tweezers which were supposed to deliver a killer frequency to the hair root. I would have a nice smooth face for a while, but it was frustrating. I didn't know how to get rid of the hair permanently.

For the next eight years, I continued cross-dressing privately, not venturing out. I had a number of relationships with women but never revealed that I liked to cross-dress. It was obvious by now that cross-dressing wasn't something that I could just wish away. There was a strong desire, a compulsion, to cross-dress. It was a part of who I was, a presentation that I liked, that of being female. I had read that some cross-dressers would occasionally do something called 'purging', getting rid of all their female clothing, being ashamed of their cross-dressing and vowing never to cross-dress again. But I never did that. Cross-dressing felt good, natural, satisfying and I enjoyed it.

Then I met a woman whom I moved in with and decided to tell her about my cross-dressing. She was to become my second wife. She had two children, a seven-year-old girl and a four-year-old boy. The children were great and I enjoyed being part of a family very much. We lived together for 2 ½ years then married for another 2 ½ years. I wanted to be open with her, so early in the relationship I brought up my cross-dressing. She pointed to her closet and said, "Help yourself." But it was obvious from the shakiness of her voice and her body language that it really wasn't okay with her. So during my relationship with her, I was again reluctant to be open about my cross-dressing. I usually did it when she was visiting with her parents, and other times when she was likely to be gone for hours.

My relationship with my second wife had been going downhill and the marriage was in trouble for a number of reasons. (Cross-dressing wasn't an issue because I kept it hidden.) Then one day she found my box of women's clothing that I kept above the garage. All hell broke loose. Suddenly, I was the pervert that she had read about in school. I never expected this kind of response, especially since I had told her about my cross-dressing in the beginning of the relationship. Well, she claimed that I had never told her! Our relationship continued to decline until I felt I had no choice but to file for a divorce. During the divorce, she tried to make me out to be gay or some sort of sexual deviant. Her attorney was attempting to use it to their advantage and intimidate me into giving them everything. In the end, it made no difference. The divorce was finalized January 1989.

A few years later, I met a very nice and understanding woman whom I gradually introduced to my cross-dressing. We enjoyed it together on a number of occasions. In fact, she helped me with makeup and got me out the front door dressed as an adult woman. We did not go anywhere significant, just out for a drive or a walk around the apartment complex, but that was a milestone for me. I enjoyed sharing my cross-dressing with her but for other reasons the relationship did not last and she started seeing someone else.

Being single and hating the fact that I had a pretty hairy body, my attention turned to my beard. My beard was very heavy and I hated shaving. So I began to investigate ways of having it removed. I was living in Dallas. After talking with a number of electrologists, I made an appointment at Electrology 2000. My first meeting with the owner was a bit confusing. He/She had long hair, a nice smooth complexion and a soft appearance, which was ambiguous. So I said, "You know, I'm not sure if you are a man or a woman." He/She appeared to be flattered by that and replied, "Thanks" with a big smile. I was confused by this response, not understanding his/her happy reaction to my uncertainty.

The approach that Electrology 2000 took was to numb the skin and use an insulated needle with only the tip bare. Numbing the skin made it possible to use a strong current to kill the hair follicle. The special needle with its insulated sides prevented scarring. They recommended a complete stripping once a month for a year. Facial hair grows in cycles, so it takes a year to treat it all. At the end of the year, I would have a very smooth face with only some minor touch-up required.

My desire to have my beard removed confused them. Straight males just didn't do that. What I did not know at the time was that their clientele consisted mostly of transsexuals, and I did not yet identify as one.

I had not heard of the term "Transgendered." I did not know that support groups existed, or that one could change their gender. What I did know was I liked to cross-dress, identified more with women, and that I wanted to get rid of my beard.

My heavy beard required a lot of time and money to remove. The computer company I worked for provided a sabbatical benefit for employees that could be taken with vacation. I took advantage of this benefit by taking a total of six consecutive weeks off from work. The first stripping took eight eight-hour days. The second stripping, a month later, took five eight-hour days. The time required decreased each month until I could do it on a Saturday, with Sunday free to allow time for the swelling to go down before work on Monday. When the year was up, I had a nice smooth hairless face with no scarring. There are a few hairs that show up on occasion and I simply remove them with tweezers.

At work, an opportunity presented itself for me to travel to San Ramon, California and assist the local office there for a few weeks. The company I worked for kept extending my stay so I ended up spending all summer there. I began to really enjoy California but the price of homes was just out of sight. "I've got to be crazy to want to move here," I thought. But when a position opened up in the San Ramon office, I applied for it and the company relocated me.

There was something special and unique about California. There was a feeling of freedom and openness that allowed me to question who I was, to want to search and seek out the truth about myself. I called the San Francisco Sex Information Hotline and learned that there were a couple of organizations in the area, ETVC (The Educational TV Channel which is now TGSF, or Transgender San Francisco) and DVG (Diablo Valley Girls). What a surprise to learn that not only were there others like myself, but there were also organizations for us. The prospect of being able to get dressed up, have someplace to go and socialize with other cross-dressers was very exciting for me.

DVG met in Walnut Creek, which was close to where I lived. They would occasionally meet at a local club. The first two socials I attended as my male self. There were perhaps twenty to thirty men, dressed as women, socializing with one another in the club. I could not believe my eyes. All my life I treated my cross-dressing as something private, not ever dreaming that there were those who were cross-dressing in public places. It wasn't until the third social that I got the courage to attend dressed as a woman. I remember it so well.

I had dressed in a blouse, skirt, bra, panties, panty hose, pumps, and long blond wig. It was scary driving to the club dressed as a woman. Would other drivers notice? Would they stare at me? What if I was involved in an accident or pulled over by the police? When I arrived at the club I found myself sitting in the parking lot trying to get up the courage to get out of the car and walk across the parking lot into the club. It was so… so very difficult. I was filled with anxiety. Cars kept coming and going, people kept coming and going. I was waiting for the parking lot to be deserted so I could get out of the car and scurry into the club without anyone seeing me.

Eventually, I did manage to get myself into the club and soon found that I was among friends. It was confusing for me in the beginning. The people there were men, so initially I used male pronouns to refer to them. Well, it was quickly and politely pointed out to me that I should refer to them using their "fem name" and female pronouns. I learned that when they dressed as women, they liked to be treated and referred to as women. When someone asked what my fem name was, well, I had not thought of that. And then someone said something about makeup and, well, I had not thought of that either. I had some work to do.

What to name my feminine self? Someone had suggested that I choose a name that starts with the same letter as my male name, James. I decided on Jeanette. Why not? I thought it had a nice sound to it. So I began introducing myself as Jeanette at the socials I attended.

It wasn't long before I had attended enough socials to make some friends. I also learned a lot more about being transgendered. Here I was, 45 years old, and just learning about who I was. In getting to know other cross-dressers, I realized that many of them, like me, also knew they were different from a very early age.

My appearance as a woman wasn't all that great and it was a concern to me. I did not want to be a man in a dress, but, rather, an attractive woman. There was one discussion with another cross-dresser that comes to mind. While I was expressing my concern over my female appearance, she posed the question: "Have you ever really looked around and noticed how many women aren't all that great looking?" Well, I must admit, I had never really thought about it that way before. Mostly I tended to compare myself to the really beautiful women instead of the average looking woman. But still, they all look female and that was a place I hadn't managed to get to yet.

The job I had was as a technical support person with a rather conservative sales group and the expectation was that I would have a clean, male, business-like appearance. This was a problem because I wanted to get my ears pierced. Clip-on earrings weren't comfortable and there was a much larger selection of earrings available if your ears were pierced. So I did it. When you get your ears pierced you are supposed to leave the piercing studs in place for about three weeks, but I couldn't do that because of my job. So, I came up with the idea to use stud sleeves, made of a clear plastic. I inserted a plastic stud sleeve into the pierced hole with some Neosporin. The Neosporin would keep the sleeve in place and also help the healing process. When I got home, I would swap the sleeves with the stud earrings. This process was repeated until my ears had healed enough that I could go to work without being concerned that the hole would close. It was so much more comfortable and fun to be out wearing pierced earrings.

There was a cross-dresser I met when I was just beginning to get out as a cross-dresser myself. She would occasionally ask if I was interested in going to a social or out to dinner and would show up as a man from time to time and treat me like a real lady. It felt great and it was an experience I will never forget. Our relationship endured as I evolved from cross-dresser to transsexual. He wanted more physically from the relationship than I was willing to give and he eventually lost interest in me. I experienced my first rejection as a woman from a man I cared about.

I owned a dog named Fritz, a sheltie collie, whom I loved dearly. We frequently went for walks together and occasionally I would drive out to a lake and we would walk the nearly three miles around it. It was daring of me and a bit scary but I would sometimes do this walk dressed as female, usually wearing shorts and some sort of long sleeve top, some makeup, earrings, sunglasses and a cap. Having fair skin, I would cover my body to protect myself from the sun. The first time Fritz and I went out walking this way I naively thought we would simply walk around the lake and that would be that. Instead, several women stopped to tell me what a beautiful dog I had. And they wanted to talk about it. It really caught me by surprise. My voice was still male and I was afraid to give myself away as a man so I just muttered something softly and got away. I continued taking Fritz for walks around the lake, dressed as female, and gradually got used to it. Outings like this helped me overcome the fear of going out in public as a woman.

I still had a pretty hairy chest and I did not like it. So I flew back to Dallas a couple of times to have electrolysis. My eyebrows were also very heavy so I had some of the thicker hairs removed. It was expensive, but I really wanted to have a more feminine appearance, so it was worth it to me.

Back home, my hair stylist used wax to remove some hair from my back. After the first waxing, the hair got thinner and after a few treatments it did not grow back. Since that worked, I was curious about waxing my eyebrows in order to get them softer and more feminine looking. That worked, as well. In fact, I wish I had not had those large hairs from my eyebrows removed using electrolysis because it resulted in a patchy eyebrow with gaps where there should have been hair. A good eyebrow pencil hides it, but if I had it to do again, I'd go with the waxing.

My job situation became precarious. The company where I had worked for 14 years laid me off in November 1995, and the following January, I started work as an independent consultant. This involved some travel. I was out of town a lot for the next nine months. While traveling, I was able to meet with other transgender groups in Omaha, Orlando, and Los Angeles.

Being among consultants, I noticed there were a number of guys with long ponytails. Long hair was something I always wanted, so I also began to grow my hair long. Eventually, I was able to find work as a consultant with a company close to where I lived. It was great to be back home and once again attend the transgender group socials I was accustomed to and be with friends.

I learned that some people were blocking their testosterone, taking female hormones and transitioning to live their lives as female. At the time, I was quite content to cross-dress and was not interested in taking hormones. But as time passed, I found myself becoming more interested in the people who were taking hormones and began to wonder whether I was a cross-dresser or a transsexual.

I noticed there weren't many transsexuals attending the socials (most people there were cross-dressers) and I was beginning to wonder why. Where were all the transsexuals? As a result of conversations with others it was becoming clear to me that, unlike other groups of people such as gays, lesbians, bisexuals and cross-dressers, transsexuals tended to stop attending support groups once they were fully transitioned as the other gender.

The fact that there were so few transsexuals attending socials made it difficult for me to benefit and learn from their experiences. It would have been great to have had the opportunity to talk to people to hear how their transitions went. Who was their therapist? Who was their doctor? Was their transition successful? Were they happier? How is their life different? What about sex? Orgasms? Better? Worse? I had so many questions, but very few people to ask. Fortunately, I heard of a transsexual support group in Berkeley. During the following year, I periodically attended it.

The support group provided me with information on hormones, problems in the work place, relationships, etc. The group endorsed a timeline for transition, in which you started hormones, transitioned to living as a woman and then culminated with SRS (Sexual Reassignment Surgery) a year later. Their schedule seemed too aggressive for me.

One concern I had was whether I could take female hormones and still get an erection. The group's response was, "You can't have your cake and eat it too." But I wasn't so sure. I had also heard that it depends on the individual.

There was also the issue of relationships. Is anyone going to want to be sexual with me? Will I find someone who loves me as a transsexual? It's scary not knowing how such a transition may turn out.

As time went on, I began to give more thought to taking hormones, what that might mean to me, the consequences, the possibility of becoming more of a woman. I felt that the time had come for me to begin seeing a therapist.

Seeing a therapist was exciting because I wanted to learn more about myself. During the next several months I read numerous books, marking passages and making lists of questions, which I would then discuss with the therapist. Over time, I began to settle in on who I was and what I wanted. The conclusion that I reached was that I was somewhere in the middle of the gender spectrum, although certainly leaning toward the female side. I figured it would suit me well to further feminize myself, even though I still had no desire for SRS.

I also came to the conclusion that I didn't like either of my names. Both James and Jeanette were too gender specific. I needed a name that was more neutral. A lady friend and I considered quite a few names but the one I liked best was Shannon. It's a name that both men and women use. As I changed, people could determine for themselves what gender I was, and the name Shannon would fit either way.

After seeing the therapist for a while, I came to the decision to have some surgery, a rhinoplasty and jaw tapering. The surgery appeared to go well but afterward I developed an infection in my jaw and had to have my nose straightened as it was a little off center. It took a long time for both my jaw and nose to heal, about two years for the swelling to go down completely. The surgeries certainly helped me achieve a more feminine facial appearance. Ironically, my next trip home, no one in my family seemed to notice.

Eventually, I requested a letter of recommendation from my therapist so I could make an appointment to see a doctor and start hormonal reassignment. As excited as I was to start the hormones, I was also afraid of the effect that they might have on my sexuality. Since I was still very much attracted to women, I was concerned about my ability to get and maintain an erection.

It was very exciting being in the doctor's office to get my hormones. The doctor asked me about children and advised me that hormonal reassignment would render me sterile after about three months and that it may not be reversible. Since I no longer had an interest in having children it was not a problem for me. She also told me to stop the electrolysis on my chest since the hormones would eliminate any chest and stomach hair. I felt sort of dumb for having had the electrolysis, but back then I was not even considering hormonal reassignment.

I was also concerned about whether or not I would even be able to appear female after transitioning. I did not want to be a man in a dress, but rather a woman. She told me that she thought I would make an attractive woman. I wasn't entirely convinced but I was hopeful that she might be correct.

What happened next was unexpected. Being male, I was definitely balding and had lost a lot of hair on the top of my head. To my surprise the doctor informed me that I could probably regain most or all of my hair. Well, that was great news! Wearing a wig is not any fun and hair plugs are expensive. The doctor said I needed to take Proscar, in addition to my hormone therapy, and a Minoxidil Retin-A combination, to stimulate the scalp and hair follicles. Nearly all of my testosterone was blocked. Recovering the hair in this way took about two years, but soon after starting my drug regimen, hair started sprouting like a newly planted lawn. It was great!

However, the first month on hormones felt very stressful. Was I doing the right thing? I was second-guessing myself, depressed at times and even having thoughts of suicide. Sexually, things felt very strained, awkward, and difficult. WAS I DOING THE RIGHT THING???

In the first month or so my libido decreased, my genitals appeared to have shed a layer of skin, and I stopped producing sperm. I got really hungry and very tired. My scalp became sensitive due to the Minoxidil Retin-A combination I was applying.

After the first month, things were much more relaxed. I was regaining my sexual function and feeling much better. My perception is that it took about thirty days for my body to adjust to the dramatic hormonal changes. Then things went more smoothly, though I was still concerned over the long-term effects this would have on my sexuality.

As I continued my hormone regimen, my skin became softer and drier, my pores got smaller and my sex drive diminished. The hair on the top of my head continued to improve. I lost muscle mass. It was most noticeable in my shoulders and feet. Eventually I stopped taking progestin as it made me very weak. My breasts began to develop and I began to experience emotions.

Emotions. Thinking back to one of the Berkeley support group meetings I had attended, I recall someone saying that the reason she had taken female hormones was for the emotions. At the time I heard this, I did not really understand it. Now I did. Emotions, at least for me, have been the biggest benefit of taking hormones. They have added a dimension to my life that was missing. It is difficult to explain, but my life now has more depth and meaning than it did before and I feel that I can relate to women much better as well. As a male, I had only been vaguely aware of emotions. Looking back, I think of myself as being emotionally dead. Now, emotions are a big part of my life. They influence every aspect of how I think, how I see the world, and how I experience life itself. Indeed, taking hormones "for the emotions" makes a lot of sense to me now. Men *think* they have emotions; women do!

Breasts. My body was really beginning to change and it meant that I was going to have to start presenting myself as female in public. I began to vary my hormone dosage up and down from what my doctor prescribed, partially to figure out if estrogen was responsible for emotions, but also because I was feeling a bit anxious about my breasts becoming noticeable. I wasn't ready for that yet. My ability to present as female needed to catch up with the physical changes that were taking place. I worried, "It's summer, it's hot, I need to go to the grocery store and I have breasts." I finally got the courage to go into the grocery store wearing a t-shirt. I was so afraid that someone might challenge me, make comments about my appearance, or even just give me dirty looks. But gradually I became accustomed to my new body and ventured out into public more confidently.

Sex Drive. For as long as I can remember, I have always had a very strong and persistent sex drive. There was almost a constant urge to masturbate and I did it often. Suppressing my testosterone and adding estrogen has lowered my sex drive to a much more manageable level. In fact, for the first time in my life, I felt in control. There was no longer this persistent urge that frequently needed to be dealt with. Instead, I could masturbate if and when I wanted to. I liked this new arrangement. It gave me more time to do other things.

One busy Saturday, I was in the gardening section of my local hardware store waiting my turn to talk to a sales clerk. There was a lady who was waiting in front of me. I was wearing a pair of sunglasses, very short jean shorts and a t-shirt. The lady occasionally glanced my way and I couldn't help but wonder what she might be thinking. Then the clerk freed up and she says to him, "Why don't you wait on this young lady first?" Wow! That was the first time I knew I was perceived as a woman in public. This experience really boosted my confidence.

At my follow-up visit with my doctor I had lots of questions and concerns, which made my doctor question whether she was doing the right thing treating me. It was always my opinion that patients should be encouraged to ask questions. So why was my doctor now suggesting that I stop taking the hormones? I left very upset, virtually in tears. So I went to my therapist, who sent a letter to my doctor indicating that she thought I was on track and should continue hormonal reassignment.

As my hair got longer and I started wearing earrings and dressing differently my neighbors eyed me with strange curiosity. There was one incident when I was walking my dog and my neighbor drove by in his Porsche. When he saw me his eyes bugged out. There was no doubt in my mind that I was beginning to be noticed by my neighbors—some were okay with it and others weren't.

After being on hormones for about seven months, I had what I believe was my first female orgasm. Instead of a typical male orgasm strong, short-lived, with an epicenter in the genital area, I found that I was experiencing waves of pleasure all over my body. Yet my priority with relationships was now becoming more about intimacy and closeness than about sex. Another surprise was that things that used to be sexually exciting for me were losing their appeal. It didn't feel like I had lost anything, though, it just felt different, actually better, than before.

It was a rather warm summer day. Fritz and I were out for a walk. There were men along the side of the road replacing sections of concrete sidewalk. One of the men yelled out, "Hey babe, you have a nice looking dog." I said, "Thank you" and kept walking. So now I'm a "babe."

It was important to me to progress at my own speed and go only as far as I felt comfortable. I was in no hurry nor did I really know just how far I would take my feminization, but I was certainly enjoying the experience. The hormone dose that I was taking felt right. I knew I could stop at any time. (There is no mandate that says you have to keep going.) I remember my therapist asking, "Have you ever thought about stopping the hormones and going back to where you were?" I quickly replied, "No, I had not even considered it." She went on to say it was obvious that I was a lot happier.

As my transition progressed, I felt there was a need to begin socializing more as a female. Women socialize differently than men and I had a lot to learn. It wasn't clear to me at first how I might do this, and then I got the idea to attend a lesbian group. And it turned out to be a good plan. The first lesbian group I attended was a rather small group of young women and even though I was 47 and transsexual, I was welcome. The time I spent with this group was really great. They would schedule social events once a month; poetry night, movie night, karaoke night, bowling, camping, and playing pool. They were a great group of women.

The second lesbian group was strictly a support group. It was a larger group consisting of about 30 to 40 women of all ages. The first time I attended, a woman who was sitting across from me said, "I don't think you belong here." I responded, "Where do you think I belong?" It was very uncomfortable. After the meeting, several other women came up to me to say that I was welcome and that she did not speak for the group. It was a relief and I felt accepted.

I also attended an outdoor women's group. One memorable outing was to Point Reyes, north of San Francisco. We hiked to a lake, went swimming, had lunch and later drove into a nearby town for dinner at a local restaurant. After dinner I needed to use the restroom. This restaurant had single occupancy restrooms for men and women and there were lines for both. Since I was not consistently passing as female and I was in a public restaurant I was not familiar with, I thought it best to get in the men's line to use the restroom. After standing there only a short time, there was a tap on my shoulder. I turned and a man began explaining to me that the women's restroom was over there. I more than willingly walked over and got in line with the women. Inside I was screaming, "YES!" I had been taken as female even though I was not really trying to be. That felt GREAT!

Prior to this, I would go places and people would be confused over my gender. For example, when I would go to the grocery store, the cashiers might say, "Thank you sir, ah ma'am, ah sir," unable to make up their mind. Once, while shopping, a manager was very confused over how to address me, unable to reconcile the difference between the name and picture on my membership card and the person who was in front of him. There was also the time I went out of town on business and after looking at my driver's license, the security guard said, "This isn't you." I replied, "Yes it is" while I let my hair down like my driver's license. It had been in a ponytail.

The gender confusion stage lasted six to twelve months. People determine gender based on different cues. Some people would immediately consider me female while others weren't sure and still others thought I was male. I enjoyed watching people attempt to figure it out and then get frustrated at not being able to do so. It was rare for me to speak up and solve the mystery for them. It has never been clear to me why gender is so important when dealing with another person. Does it really matter? Can't we treat people as individuals? I am Shannon. Do you really need to know my gender in order to communicate with me and treat me with the respect that I deserve as a human being?

My parents lived in Kentucky. My mother began visiting me frequently while I was in California, initially staying a week or so then staying longer and longer with each trip until she was staying about three weeks. We began to develop a close relationship. I think the estrogen I was taking made it easier for me to relate to and understand her. When she ended up in the hospital's critical care unit, I flew out to help her. She was experiencing discomfort in her abdominal area. The doctors found numerous tumors. Cancer had invaded her gut.

After my mother had recovered from the surgery, she sent me a card and it was this card that made me so aware of the emotions I now possessed. As James, I do believe that I would have simply read the card and thought it nice, but as Shannon, I *felt* the words. I felt the emotional impact of those words and the feelings that my mother might have been experiencing when she picked out that card to send me. For the first time in my life I felt an emotional surge and I cried. That card will always have very special meaning for me.

My contract as a consultant ended. It was becoming increasingly important for me to have a stable home where I could develop relationships. So I began looking for full-time work near where I lived.

Luckily, I found a job but the commute was a long one. So I started looking for a new home and the following December moved to Felton, California. This move provided an ideal time for me to start a new life as a female and that is exactly what I did. I introduced myself to people as Shannon. However, at my new job, I still went by James, since Shannon was not my legal name.

A couple of months after I moved, I unexpectedly met a young lady with whom I became romantically involved. I still didn't know whether I could be successful in relationships with women. One evening, we went for a walk and she told me she did not know whether I was a man or a woman. Later, I decided to share with her that I was a male-to-female transsexual. We were at my home, in the living room. It was the first time I had come out to someone I really cared about. I was so afraid that she would then want to have nothing to do with me.

She listened intently, taking in every word. Afterward, she was overwhelmed, searching for the right words to say, attempting to deal with her emotions. It wasn't clear to me whether she was angry, shocked, or didn't understand what I had said. But then she began to speak with love and compassion in her voice. She respected how I pursued what was important to me, how honest and in touch I must be with myself. She felt honored that I had shared such a personal thing with her. She said that she honestly had not known if I was a man or a woman. She wanted to know if my male genitals were intact. I said yes and she was glad. After this experience, I felt so good about myself and the transition I was undergoing. She had accepted me for who I was and that meant the world to me. We became very close after that.

My relationship with her was very different. It wasn't about sex. It was a close friendship. Sex came later and it was great! The sexual urge was no longer focused in my genital area. Instead, I was having good feelings all over. There was this intense satisfaction from being emotionally close to her.

Being Shannon and James got confusing and tiresome after a while. People I knew would call me at work expecting Shannon to answer the phone and hear James instead. And when I called people I knew outside of work from my workplace, I was Shannon on the phone. I couldn't help but wonder what my co-workers were thinking! This went on for over a year. Then Thanksgiving 2000 came and I decided that the time had come to change my name (but not my gender) at the office.

I walked into my manager's office and asked if I could change my first name on my company ID card from James to Shannon and, to my surprise, he said, "Sure." So I went to the Human Resources Department and requested the change. I got my new ID card the next day, asked our security administrator, who was very supportive, about changing my name for email and was informed that it could easily be done. Next, I sent out an email to all my co-workers announcing my name change. I then received an email from my manager asking if the name change was legal. I replied no and that I had already sent out an email informing everyone about the change. It was left at that. My co-workers started using my new name as soon as they read the email and within a couple of days, almost everyone was using my new name.

There were some co-workers, however, who had a more difficult time with the name change and would inadvertently continue to call me James. Mostly, they were people I worked closely with. There was talk, and there were questions as to why I had changed my name. My typical response was the fact that I never did like the name "James." Some thought that I was changing my gender, but I wasn't, at least not yet. Immediately after my name change there were a couple of emails that referred to me using female pronouns.

My relationship lasted about a year, nine months of that being great. The reasons the relationship ended were never clear to me. There was the stigma about being thought a lesbian which she did not like. And, no doubt, she had other reasons. The ending of this relationship affected me more than any other I can remember. Possibly because it was the strongest emotional connection I had ever felt with another person. This breakup, the recent loss of my mother, and the loss of my dog soon after, threw me into a deep depression. It would take over a year for me to come out of it.

When the time seemed right, I decided to *legally* change my name from James to Shannon. To get the process started, I went to the law library located in the basement of the county court house. The librarian helped me identify which forms were required for my name change and how to complete them. The cost to me was the cost of the copies, 25 cents each. So for $1.50 I had all the legal forms I needed. My next step was to go upstairs to the superior court clerk office to submit the forms and request a court date. This step required a legal fee of $191. There was also a requirement to advertise my intent to change my name in the local paper for at least four weeks prior to the court date. A court date was set for about six weeks out. My next stop was to the local paper to place the ad for four weeks, which cost $57. This was all very exciting for me.

My court date came and I was nervous. What would the judge ask me? Would I be interrogated? Would anyone really care? I didn't know what to expect. When the door to the courtroom was unlocked, I walked in and waited for my name to be called. My petition was last on the court's docket. The judge asked, "Are you James?" I said "yes" and he signed the court order. Then back to the superior court clerk office to get three certified copies of the court order for my name change, which cost $24. The total cost had been about $275. And that was that!

I headed to the social security office and the DMV. I was only focusing on the name change, with plans to change my gender later.

Then came the arduous process of changing my name with everyone I did business with. For the most part it wasn't a problem. (However, it took *forever* to get the airlines to change the name on the promotional stuff they send out!) An insurance company wanted a certified copy of the court order. The mortgage company charged $25 to change the name on my home loan.

It was time to have my car's oil changed. The previous visit, I had them change my name from James to Shannon. For some reason, James came up again and I was asked if James was my husband. I simply explained that I had changed my name to Shannon and did not know why James was showing up. The man behind the counter changed it to Shannon without comment.

A similar thing happened to me at Radio Shack. As I was checking out at the register, they asked for personal information and their computer came back with a James at my address so they asked, "Is James your husband?" I went along with it and said, "Yes." Now I have a husband, so to speak.

My mother passed away before I started living as female. It's sort of ironic that my mother had always wanted a girl and I can't help but wonder what she would have thought of my transition. She was a very loving person and more than anything she loved her children. No doubt she noticed changes in my appearance and I am sure that even though she would have missed James, she would have continued to love Shannon.

My father was 76 years old and I decided not to tell him because I wanted to spare him the anxiety that he might experience. It was unlikely that he would understand and he might blame himself or worry about me. He would certainly worry for my safety.

Later he inadvertently discovered that I had changed my name to Shannon. After an upsetting discussion he removed me from my position as executor of his will and disowned me. I called him the following Thanksgiving hoping to patch things up but he refused to even acknowledge me by repeatedly saying, "Who? Who?" into the phone.

One afternoon while attending a work-related training, I found myself alone with another woman. We were talking about her children, two boys, and how that was fine with her because she always wanted boys. I was telling her my mother had four boys and always wanted a girl when she interrupted saying, "And then she had you!" I was a bit embarrassed when I realized what had happened. I said, "No, I am the oldest." She looked at me puzzled. Then I explained that I was transsexual and she started asking questions about hormones and surgery. I was surprised and relieved that she perceived me as female.

Previously, I had come out to several women and a couple of men in the office. The women were very supportive and had lots of questions. The men didn't seem to care. One day I was sharing some pictures I had taken on a recent trip when I suddenly realized that there might be pictures of me as female in the stack. Quickly, I grabbed the pictures and went through them muttering something like there were some pictures of my other self that I wanted to remove. My co-worker looked at me and said, "I have a neighbor like you." And I said, "What do you mean?" She replied, "He is also in the process of changing." Realizing that she knew, I let her see all the pictures. When she got to the pictures of me as female she said, "You look pretty good." We talked and I was impressed with just how much she knew about the MTF transition process and I was especially surprised because I had thought of her as being a rather conservative person who might not embrace me.

Another time I came out to two co-workers while out of town. We were sightseeing together and had stopped for lunch. They started talking about someone who was bisexual. I said, "I didn't know that." Then one of them said, "So what's going on with you?" This caught me by surprise. I engaged in a little conversation to determine whether I should tell them or not, sort of feel them out. They seemed genuinely interested, so I told them that I was transsexual. One of them mentioned when she had first seen me, she thought the company had hired a female systems administrator. Then she found out my name was James. They had questions and we had some fun talking about the ins and outs of being transsexual. They were both very supportive and thought that I should go ahead and transition at work… what was I waiting for? It was time for me to seriously consider transitioning from male-to-female on the job, but I was afraid of being discriminated against or even losing my job.

Due to recent changes in the law, which required the DMV to crosscheck a person's social security number, name, and gender with the Social Security Database, I had to first change my gender with the Social Security office. They accepted the DMV form which my doctor had signed indicating that I had undergone hormonal, but not surgical, reassignment. Two weeks later, I changed my gender with the DMV using the same form. I was rather nervous but it was handled like any other business transaction. The man at the DMV who processed my request had to have his supervisor come over and provide access in order to make the gender change. It was business as usual for them.

As I spent more time contemplating the transition at work, another issue presented itself. I had been on high doses of hormones for five years now. The recommendation is two or three years. SRS did not appeal to me, yet I needed to get off the high hormone dosages I was taking. It was obvious that I had no intention of going back to being a man and my testes did tend to get in the way a lot. So the obvious thing to me was to have a bilateral orchiectomy. This is a surgical procedure in which the testes are removed. With them gone, a major source of testosterone is eliminated, which meant that I could stop taking my testosterone blocker and also significantly lower my estrogen dose. It was February and I was due a tax refund, which would cover the cost of the operation.

After mulling over just how I would transition on the job, I came across the Center for Gender Sanity. This organization provides support for people who are transitioning on the job. They provided me with a list of actions I could take to better ensure that my transition was successful. I did a lot of preparation, everything from putting into writing what I was going to say to having photos of what I would look like when I came to the office as a female. The Center for Gender Sanity had two books on work transitions, which I purchased, read, and later loaned to Human Resources (HR). I felt it was important to portray myself as being genuine and prepared.

I also involved my therapist in the process both for my benefit and in the event my employer might want to consult with her. She gave me valuable feedback about my appearance, offered helpful suggestions, engaged in role plays to help me visualize how the transition might go, and helped me cope with the anxiety and fear that I had about it.

Most of my female clothes were either casual or really dressy for going out to clubs (from my cross-dressing days). The clothes I needed now were for the office. Luckily, two women from work offered to go shopping with me. Shopping wasn't something I knew much about, especially shopping for women's clothes. I found it very valuable to go with a woman because I learned much about where to go, how to shop, what might look good on me, do's and don'ts. It was fun.

The day came when all the preparations were complete and I was ready to contact HR about transitioning. The HR manager sat behind her desk smiling at me. I felt safe and comfortable as I began to explain why I was there. We chatted for a moment and then I communicated my intention. She asked a few questions such as when I was wanting to transition and what my recommendations were for restroom use. She said that she would review the two books I had given her and get back to me the following week. Prior to ending the meeting, I told her that I did not want to lose my job, that if this was going to cause a problem or if HR and management did not feel that they could support my gender change, that I did not want to do it. She was professional and reassuring.

When she contacted me again, we had a short meeting. She told me she had met with the Vice President of HR. They had agreed that I could show up for work as female on April 29th and that they wanted me to use the single occupancy restroom for 90 days, after which time they would take another look at my restroom use. This plan seemed good. It would get me out of the men's restroom and allow a 90-day period for the women to get used to me as female and then allow me use of the women's restrooms. We also discussed scheduling a meeting with co-workers in my immediate work group.

As it turned out, the meeting with my co-workers was scheduled for the day I had committed to a radio interview, so I did not attend the meeting. It had always been my intention to speak to the group directly and I felt guilty for dumping that responsibility on the HR manager. But the meeting seemed to go well. The only question being which restroom I would be using.

After a visit with my therapist, I felt much better. On Monday morning, April 29th, as I got ready for work, dressing in female clothes, I felt okay, almost calm. Living as female outside of work prior to transitioning at work had helped prepare me for this day. I was already used to wearing female clothes and going out in public as female. The only difference today was that I was going to work. So off I went. I walked into the office as a confident woman and was only a little anxious. I wore a black floral skirt and a black knit top. My hair was nice and curly since I had braided it the night before. Arriving at my cubicle, I took a deep breath and began to relax. I had managed to take another big step toward being the woman I always wanted to be.

189

I decided to go around and touch base with people in the office. It was important to me that they knew I was okay with my new presentation and I wanted them to be comfortable with it as well. I didn't want anyone to be afraid to talk to me; after all, I am the same person. I got some interesting looks and lots of smiles. After one of my female co-workers gave me a couple of strange looks, I went over and asked, "Are you okay with this?" She turned to me and said with a smile, "You know, you actually look pretty good."

The support and acceptance I got was overwhelming. One lady in the office brought me a rose, remembering I had mentioned that I liked roses. Another woman asked me how it was going and gave me a big hug. There were a number of women in the office who stood up to those who denounced or criticized my gender change. The men didn't say much, with one exception. There was one man who approached me and expressed his support for my gender change and was curious about it. We talked at length. Needless to say, I was impressed with his openness, acceptance and support.

Unfortunately, I did experience some negativity and discrimination. There was a guy who told my friend that he/she/it (referring to me) was going to Hell. Then I overheard a few guys who were condemning me for what I had done. And there was a co-worker who was tasked with helping me cross-train onto a new computer platform who claimed it wasn't in his job description to do so. He would also undermine me whenever the opportunity arose. Finally, there were the Christian co-workers in another state who wouldn't return my phone calls or reply to my emails.

Having survived the transition at work, I now live full-time as a woman. I feel so much better and my anxiety is much lower than it was prior to transitioning on the job.

My aunt lives near Tampa, Florida and I have always considered her to be a very accepting person, much like my mother. My mother's death brought us back together after many years of being apart. We started talking on the phone and after a few months I told her what was going on with me, my being transsexual and all that went with it. She was very accepting and has since been very supportive. She and her husband had some difficulty visualizing me as female until I sent them some photos. The photos gave them something tangible to see and made it real for them that I was indeed female. Now they both accept and support me as Shannon.

It has been four years now since I started hormonal reassignment. Prior to this, I can remember so many times when I looked at myself in the mirror and thought, there is no way that I am ever going to pass as female, and felt so sad about it. I wanted so much to have a female appearance. Today, I find myself looking in the mirror and saying to myself, this is really going to work. The image that I see in the mirror is that of a woman. Something I never thought I was going to be able to accomplish really did happen.

It is rare now that I am referred to as male. People perceive me and accept me as female. My sexual orientation is lesbian, meaning that I am attracted to women sexually. My breasts are now overflowing an A cup, a baby B. I have soft skin, long hair, lots of emotions, and can still get an erection.

My voice, at times, gives me away as being male. Acquiring a more feminine voice has been very difficult. I started seeing a hypnotist for help with weight and I just happened to mention that I was having a difficult time developing a feminine voice. I really didn't expect her to be able to help me, but through hypnosis she helped me come up with the incentive to work harder at making my voice more feminine. It was surprising just how much that helped. The next thing I knew I was singing with Celine Dion and my voice was changing. People now frequently tell me how much they like my voice and that they think it sounds feminine to them, but, unfortunately, when I am talking on the phone I still get "Mr." and "Sir" a lot. It would appear that I still have more work to do in achieving a true feminine voice (although I have been told by some women that they are frequently sir'd on the phone, too).

My relationships with men and women have changed. Both sexes engage me more. Men tend to relate to me as a female, which I have found most interesting, and I am welcomed and accepted by women. I have more friends and social contacts today than I have ever had.

There is a man in my life now. He is about 30 years my senior. I first met him while roaming through the redwoods. He knows me only as female and is a dear friend. We have common interests and frequently do things together. He treats me as a woman ought to be treated and is a very honest and respectful person with lots of integrity. This man has earned my trust and respect and, at least for the interim, I share my home with him. We enjoy each other's company very much.

When I started hormonal reassignment years ago, my desire was to be physically female. What I got was so much more. The female hormones have affected me in so many ways, physically, mentally, sexually, emotionally and have affected my behavior, perception, awareness, and relationships. I got much more than I had expected and am ever so thankful.

The emotions that came with hormonal reassignment have made it possible for me to experience life in a new way. The beauty of nature is more appreciated and felt. My relationships with people are more genuine as I relate more to the person inside. I am more in touch with my surroundings and my feelings. Of course, I have my emotional days now that I am a woman, something I didn't have to cope with as a man.

The biggest thing is that I am now the person I have always wanted to be. I am no longer longing to be the other gender. It's a huge relief to be free of that burden and constant yearning.

There have also been some not so great changes. The most significant one is that I don't have the strength or stamina that I had as a man. It takes more effort to do physical things and getting into shape and staying in shape takes more effort than it used to. I bruise more easily. My doctor reminds me that I am older and while that may have contributed to the decrease in my physical abilities, in my heart I know that the hormones are the major contributing factor.

As a man I always felt that I had to be doing something. Now my drive, my motivation, is not what it used to be. It's easier for me to just sit back, relax and do nothing, so I have to push myself at times to get things done. I tire more easily and seem to require more sleep. Again, my doctor would probably remind me that this is age related. I am not so sure.

Another change I have noticed is that I don't feel as safe when I'm alone. I am less likely to be walking in the woods after sunset or feel comfortable walking downtown alone. Generally I feel that I have to be more aware of my surroundings and not as carefree as I used to be.

And lastly, it takes more effort to be a woman. There are many mornings when I wake up and have no idea what I am going to wear.

While I enjoy the variety of clothes that I can now wear, it does take some effort to put it all together. And then there is putting on makeup and fixing my hair every morning. But I can't really complain. I like wearing the clothes, the makeup, and even the uncomfortable shoes. But more than anything, I enjoy being a woman.

The one thing that comes to mind when I look back at my transition is how smooth it was. Yes, there were times when it was stressful, such as the first time I got out of my car as female and walked into a club, or the first month I was on hormones or transitioning on the job. But overall, my transition has been smoother than I ever thought it would be. I think that was because I took my time. I never pushed myself to transition faster than I was ready. Changing gender is not a trivial task. There is a lot that needs to change physically, emotionally and behaviorally and it takes time.

Having lived as both male and female, it is my personal opinion that it's easier being a man, but more rewarding being a woman.

Addendum

The Harry Benjamin Standards of Care define the route for persons wishing to change their gender. They also guide professionals in the treatment of "gender identity disorder" which is the diagnosis in the Diagnostic and Statistical Manual of Mental Disorders (DSM) that pertains to being transgendered. The Standards of Care include such steps as having a diagnostic assessment, going through psychotherapy, and obtaining "real life experience" in one's preferred gender role, followed by hormone therapy and surgery.

While the Standards of Care are intended to help transgendered people and clinicians by providing guidance, many people disagree with the process, finding it doesn't fit their circumstances. For example, some people start changing their gender before they seek professional help. Some people are insulted by the requirement to see a psychotherapist when they feel quite clear, mentally healthy and capable of making their own decisions. Others find they can't have "real life experience" until after they have hormone therapy and/or surgery.

About the Editors

Marsea Marcus is a licensed marriage and family counselor who specializes in eating disorders and body image issues. She is the co-author with Andrea Wachter of *The Don't Diet, Live-It Workbook*, a book about recovering from eating disorders. Marsea's life-partner is a female-to-male transsexual who transitioned in 1974, when he was 18. They met in 1994 and have been together ever since.

Shannon Weckman holds three degrees: an A.S. in Radiologic Technology, a B.S. in Computer Science and an MBA. She has written articles for transgender newsletters, been a guest speaker on the radio, and been a trainer and speaker for Triangle Speaker's transgender program and community outreach. Shannon is a male-to-female transsexual. In 1996, at age 44, she began her transition, which she completed in 2002.

CPSIA information can be obtained at www.ICGtesting.com
Printed in the USA
BVOW081601280911

272358BV00014B/99/P